THE EUCHARIST

THE EUCHARIST

E. SCHILLEBEECKX, O.P.

translated by N. D. Smith

SHEED AND WARD - New York

Contents

THE EUCHARIST

Alarm over
New Interpretations

A COMPLETELY NEW theological interpretation of the eucharistic presence arose in the thirteenth century in reaction to
the "sensualistic" interpretation of the quite unique presence
of Christ in the Eucharist ("in communion, I really bite the
true body of Christ") which had been generally prevalent,
although not accepted entirely without criticism, in the
Middle Ages. This new interpretation was advocated by, for
example, Albert the Great, Bonaventure and Thomas, to
name only the leading figures, and it certainly contained an
element of shock. It could not, however, cause alarm in the
pastoral sphere, since the ordinary people in the Middle
Ages had no idea at all of what was happening in the
universities. Despite these "modernists," most people in the
Church continued to think about the Eucharist in a way
that had already been in existence for centuries and had been
brought about largely by the great Pope Gregory I, whose
influence on medieval spirituality had been immense and
who had, to a great extent, been responsible for giving it its
moving naivety.

This "new theology" of the thirteenth century, sounding

so very new and modernist and apparently penetrating to the very heart of the Christian faith, would undoubtedly have caused great alarm in our twentieth-century "open system" of society, with its press and other means of communication, and above all with its constant stream of ideas flowing from above to below and from below to above and its many cross-channels interconnecting the whole of modern "mixed society." Bonaventure's attitude towards the traditional ideas seems to have been distinctly provocative—"Thoughtless persons put forward all kinds of ideas in this sacrament that are really dangerous."[1] The naive traditional conception of the Eucharist was often too much even for Thomas. There were, he said, Christians who thought that whenever unbelievers pricked consecrated hosts, in hatred or a desire to inflict torture, and the hosts began, according to the medieval legends, to bleed, this "blood" was really the true blood of Christ. Thomas was unable to accept this gross realism. Although he believed in these miracles, he nonetheless said that whatever the blood might have been,

[1] Bonaventure, *In IV Sent.,* d. 10, pars II, a. 2, q. 1; edn. Quaracchi, pt. 4, p. 236 B. A good survey of the current views on the Eucharist from the sixth to the end of the eleventh century will be found in J. Geiselmann, *Die Eucharistie-Lehre der Vorscholastik,* Paderborn (1926) and of the early scholastic views (that is, the twelfth century and the beginning of the thirteenth) in A. Landgraf, *Dogmengeschichte der Frühscholastik,* pt. III-2, Ratisbon (1955), especially pp. 207–22, H. Jorissen, *Die Entfaltung der Transsubstantiationslehre bis zum Beginn der Hochscholastik,* Münster (1965) and L. Hödl, "Der Transsubstantiationsbegriff in der scholastischen Theologie des 12. Jahrhunderts," *Rech. Théol. Anc. Méd.* 21 (1964), pp. 230–59. See also H. de Lubac, *Corpus Mysticum,* Paris (1944).

it was certainly not Christ's blood.[2] He even went so far as to maintain that Christ was not enclosed in the tabernacle, although the sacramental forms or consecrated hosts were present there.[3] The species realised the "physical presence" of Christ for us, but they did this "in a spiritual—that is, invisible—manner."[4] All the "new theologians" were in complete agreement about one thing—Christ did not transfer his dwelling from heaven to the altar, and he did not make himself small so as to "conceal" himself in a mysterious manner in the consecrated hosts.[5] What is more, Thomas continued, we must take care when we speak of the "substance of the bread," since bread was a product of cultivation[6] and its "substance" came about as the result of baking a dough made from flour and water (*ibid.*). He warned us therefore not to make any mystery of this, although he conceded that the material world was the basis on which, by human intervention, this new substance was produced (*ibid.*).

Did these modernists then not accept the "real presence"?

[2] Thomas, *ST*, III, q. 76, a. 8, c. and ad 2. Stories of Jesus' appearances "in the host" were well known in the ninth century and, at the end of the twelfth and the beginning of the thirteenth centuries, there were many stories going around about the "bleeding" of the host and the red colouring of the consecrated white wine. See P. Browe, "Die eucharistischen Verwandlungswunder des Mittelalters," *Röm. Quartalschr.* 37 (1929), pp. 137–69 and "Die scholastische Theorie der eucharistischen Verwandlungswunder," *Tüb. Theol. Quartalschr.* 110 (1929), pp. 305–32.

[3] *ST*, III, q. 76, a. 7, c.

[4] *ST*, III, q. 75, a. 1, ad 4.

[5] *ST*, III, q. 75, a. 2; III, q. 83, a. 4, ad 9.

[6] *ST*, III, q. 75, a. 6, ob. 1 and ad 1: "quiddam artificiale."

Did they not shock the traditional faith of the pious Middle Ages? They even went so far as to criticise the Roman Synod which, earlier, had submitted a profession of faith concerning the eucharistic presence to the heretic Berengarius. In Bonaventure's opinion, this *professio fidei* was "excessively formulated" and exaggeratedly sensualistic.[7] Thomas also attacked its formulation,[8] saying that we do not crush Christ with our teeth—"Christ is not eaten and chewed with the teeth in his corporeality, but in sacramental forms." Thus, in an urbane way, he gave a non-

---

[7] "Quamvis nimis expressa": see Bonaventure, *In IV Sent.*, d. 12, pars I, a. 3, q. 1, p. 284 A. For Berengarius, see P. Engels, "De eucharistieleer van Berengarius van Tours," *Ts. V. Theol.* 5 (1965), pp. 363–392.

[8] Denzinger 355 (700) only quotes the *professio fidei*. Thomas knew the whole text (already changed by polemics), III, q. 77, a. 7, ob. 3, via the *Decretum Gratiani*, P. 3, d. 2, can. 42 (see edn. Richter-Friedberg, pt. 1, col. 1328). This Roman Synod of 1059, held under Pope Nicholas II, said, among other things: "Consentio autem sanctae romanae Ecclesiae et Apostolicae Sedi . . . et ore et corde profiteor panem et vinum quae in altari ponuntur, post consecrationem verum corpus et sanguinem Christi esse, *et sensualiter, non solum sacramento, sed in veritate, manibus sacerdotum tractari, et frangi et fidelium dentibus atteri*" ("I accept the Holy Roman Church and the Apostolic See . . . and with my lips and my heart I profess that the bread and wine which are placed on the altar are after consecration the body and blood of Christ, and *sensualiter, not only sacramentally but in reality, are handled by the priest and broken and crushed by the teeth of the faithful*"); see Mansi, pt. 19, col. 900— hence the word "sensualism" (the idea emerges clearly from the italicised text). Other Roman synods under Gregory VII only took over the real *professio fidei*, as, for example, did the Fifth Roman Synod of 1078 (see Mansi, pt. 20, col. 516) and the Sixth of 1079 (see Mansi, pt. 20, col. 524). There had for a long time been a reaction against the anti-Berengarian "sensualism."

sensualistic explanation of the document.[9] To allay the "sensory temptations" of priests who drank the consecrated wine and then apparently became tortured by uncertainty because they tasted wine and not blood, he gave the assurance that what they tasted was no deceit[10]—what they drank was "a *sacramentum* of Christ's blood."[11] Bonaventure called them "the forms of the most holy signs."[12]

Compared with the rather sensualistic way in which ordinary members of the Church and the priests who guided them interpreted the eucharistic presence in the Middle Ages, these ideas must all have been quite shocking! But the *fides maiorum* was able to exist peacefully beside this *fides minorum* in the Middle Ages.[13] Anyone who had, for example, attended the *facultas artium* or studied *Sacra Doctrina* (the theological faculty) in Paris, Cologne or Oxford had in fact an idea of the faith that was completely different from the "sensualistic" experience of faith of the

---

[9] See *ST*, III, q. 77, a. 7, ad 3: "Illud quod manducatur in propria specie, ipsummet frangitur et masticatur in sua specie. Corpus autem Christi non manducatur in sua specie, sed in specie sacramentali. . . . Et *hoc modo* intelligenda est confessio Berengarii. . . ." ("That which is eaten in its own species, the same is broken and masticated in its own species. But the body of Christ is not eaten in its own, but in sacramental, species. . . . And *in this sense* the profession of Berengarius is to be understood. . . .").

[10] *ST*, III, q. 75, a. 5, ad 2.

[11] *ST*, III, q. 77, a. 7: "*sacramentum* corporis Christi veri."

[12] Bonaventure, *In IV Sent.*, d. 9, a. 2, q. 1, ad 5, p. 508 B: "species sanctissimorum symbolorum."

[13] The *fides maiorum* had, after all, the function of interpreting the *fides implicita* of the ordinary people in the Church in the Middle Ages.

ordinary people in the Church. This average experience of faith pursued its calm and undisturbed course—and with a fundamentally authentic Catholic meaning—after the time of these great innovators (who had themselves continued the work of the early scholastics) and has even persisted to the present day. The basic meaning of the "scientific faith" of these "new theologians" was in the final analysis precisely the same as that of the ordinary faithful of the Church. But what a difference in the two ways of representing the faith!

Although this "scientific faith" certainly appeared to be more subtly nuanced, it seemed to lack something of the basic feeling of the "faith of the people," which always contained the awareness that sacramentality is there precisely in order to give us a firm hold on reality, to put heart into us. An extreme example of this is perhaps the faith of the Curé d'Ars, who was as "sensualistic" in his attitude as the simple people and could look at the sacred host for hours in prayer and say, "Je Le vise et Il me vise"—"We are looking at each other." Not everyone is able to experience the mystery in this way—eucharistic piety is subject to a certain *metabletica,* the possibilities of which are provided inwardly by the virtualities of the *sacramentum,* as the making sensible and visible of real saving events.

Historia, magistra vitae! A close look at the Christian past always brings profound calm to the life of faith in the midst of the fevered search for new interpretations. Our faith subsists in historicity. The situational factor is certainly more productive of tensions today than in the past—the situation is even explosive. Faith is, thank God, no longer simply a question for those who are theologians. In our time faith and theology have become news for the press, and this has led to the development of a *new ethical situation* for the theologian. He can no longer pursue his theological inquiries in detachment from the question of how ordinary people in the Church are going to interpret what he has written. The fact that this new interpretation must perhaps be regarded as necessary is not the final thing to be considered. The new ethical situation lays upon the theologian the obligation of so formulating the new interpretation—bearing in mind all the difficulties and patiently taking into account religious sensibilities, which today tend to be closely bound up with "key words," "points of reference" and "familiar images"—that the Catholic faithful may be enabled to recover their deepest insights concerning the faith and may not be simply shocked. He must also beware of giving any cause for enthusiastic disciples heedlessly abandoning the deepest Catholic sense of the faith simply because they have missed the point of the new and "obvious" interpretation.

It is of course true that alarm can never be avoided entirely and that the fear of causing a certain amount of disturbance is no reason for remaining silent. No one can foresee *all* the reactions—justified and unjustified—there will be to what he says or writes. But our contemporary situation demands that the practice of theology should be carried on in a genuinely ascetical way as a work of mercy. If this is not his attitude, the theologian, whose aim must be to make the mystery or the dogmas of faith *speak* to us in our life here and now, will have missed his finest opportunities and in

fact have repudiated the basic intention with which he set
out. For then only one impression will be left in the minds
of many believers—*That* makes sense to us. Whether the
facet they have seized belongs to the sense of the faith which
has been cherished since time immemorial, the ancient history of man which began like a new springtime at the Last
Supper, seems to some people to be purely incidental. They
are concerned with the impression they gain from reading—
an impression that is usually wrong. But how shall we assign
a cause for this?

Another reaction is also unjustifiable in the *Christian*
sense—namely, the attitude that here we are confronted with
a deep *mystery* of faith, before which we must bow our
heads in worship and let the tongue of our proud theology
be silent! This is entirely wrong! Bowing our heads in worship before the mystery of salvation stimulates thought about
the faith, precisely because we believe in a *mystery,* and not
in nonsense or abracadabra. As Thomas rightly said (and
hereby he was only formulating the whole tradition of faith,
and even anticipating Bultmann's *Vorverständnis,* "pre-
understanding"): "Man cannot give consent in faith to what
is proposed to him unless he *to some extent understands
it*"—there can be no faith without Vorverständnis![14] *In* the
mystery, revelation presents itself as *full of meaning* because

---

[14] *ST,* II–II, q. 8, a. 8, ad 2: "non enim posset homo assentire credendo
aliquibus propositis, nisi ea aliqualiter intelligeret." Thomas was speaking
here of genuine "pre-understanding": "Fides *non potest* universaliter"—
"all along the line"—"*praecedere* intellectum: non enim posset homo
assentire credendo nisi . . ." (*ibid.*).

it is *full of being*. True worship is not the nonsensical attitude summed up in the quip "I believe in everything the
Church proposes to me, true or false!" Worship has everything to gain from an *existential* dimension of human life.
All my existential experience in thinking about myself and
in thinking myself through is confronted with this sacred
mystery. It is bound up with it. The Johannine gospel is
one long prayerful meditation on the part of the Church
concerning the celebration of the Eucharist, and the en-
thusiasm of the Church's celebration can still be savored
afterwards *in* theological speculation, for if revelation has
become "theology" anywhere, it is in the gospel of St. John!

Therefore the discussion of transubstantiation can have its
fullest meaning only if it is placed within the whole context
of the liturgical sacramental event. But that would mean
that this book would become a trilogy. So I must unwill-
ingly limit myself—and objections to this will be legitimate
—to a specified analysis of transubstantiation as such. Circumstances compel me to this course even though as a theologian I think a treatment of this kind methodologically
wrong. With this in mind, however, I will try to deal as best
I can with the risks involved.

What seems to me to be a basic methodological fault in
many modern attempts to interpret dogma precisely as
Catholic dogma is the fact that it is interpreted from a modern phenomenological standpoint without making clear
what the dogma of, for example, the Council of Trent demands of one as a believing Catholic. But this seems to me
to be the very first question that should be asked—What

does God's word of revelation, in the Church's authoritative interpretation, tell me about the eucharistic event? I do not in the least mean to claim that one ought to start out by putting one's own contemporary ideas "in brackets" in order to establish in the first place precisely what was revealed, and only then to interpret it in a contemporary manner. That would simply be impossible. My contemporary ideas are bound to be indissociable from my research into what the Tridentine dogma, for example, means to us. Any attempt to put the modern problem "into brackets" would *a priori* prevent me from precisely interpreting the dogmatic content. The medieval interpretation of the mystery of faith was not a problem for the medieval theologian, but it is for me, living in a different world of ideas. I cannot appreciate at its true value the dogmatic significance of the Council of Trent—a historical closeup set in a history that is constantly moving forward—if I act as though history had ceased to move forward since Trent; as though I, still as a believing Catholic, had not become, as a twentieth-century man, a different person from medieval man, even as a believer; and as though the Catholic faith had remained outside the progress of history. If this were so, faith would not be a *living* faith. Indeed, it would no longer be *faith* at all, since faith is of its nature an existential event. My faith, in this case, would simply be concerned with monuments and documents and not with God's eschatological act of salvation which revealed itself to us *in* history as *Theos pros hèmas* (as the Greek fathers were always saying)—as God for us in the man Jesus the Christ, the Son of God. What is more, I shall never be able to grasp the full meaning of the event of salvation *as it addresses me objectively* if I accept simply a history of mankind and forget that grace itself also makes history and is history and can only be a reality for me in historicity, *the* reality of my life.

But, however fascinating they may be, we must leave these formalising considerations on one side and, as twentieth-century believers, look for the *objective* meaning of the Tridentine dogma. The formalising considerations are certainly present, in the manner of living experience, in this concrete search, which is often less deterring and more easily understood than a hermeneutic thematisation. I propose to do no more than this in the first chapter of this book, as it is, in my opinion, the first requirement from the theological and methodological point of view. In the second chapter, I shall try to interpret the reality of faith of the distinctive real presence of Christ in the Eucharist in a manner that is open to the experience of modern man and above all as an authentic Catholic dogma which every Catholic can accept and with which he can feel at home even in the new climate of thought of the twentieth century.

I

The Tridentine Approach
to Faith

The General Background

WE KNOW from the whole history of theology that it is always dangerous simply to repeat a formulation of faith which was made in a different climate of thought in the past and that if we do so it is hardly possible to speak of a *living* affirmation of faith. According to the Constitution on Revelation, it is impossible to grasp the real biblical meaning of Scripture without a knowledge of the various literary genres and the distinctive forms of thought of the writers of the Old and New Testaments. What theologians openly apply to Scripture, which is inspired, they must just as openly venture to apply to conciliar statements. What is remarkable, however, is that some Christians show more reverence for these statements than they do for the Bible. Nevertheless we must persevere in putting this method into practice if we are to be faithful to God's revealing word. We should be failing in reverence for the word of God if we were simply to put forward our own limited interpretations and representations as the norm for the authentic faith of our fellow-Christians.

On the other hand, however, we can never find the word of God anywhere in its pure state. Phrases like "the wording of the dogma," as opposed to its essence, although they may be quite correctly applied in a *retrospective* situation, are fundamentally misleading. They give the impression that we can dress a dogma up in words and strip it of its words with the ease of a child playing at dressing and undressing a doll. In the thought of a past age concerning the faith, which may be for us *now* an outmoded way of thinking, it is possible for us to make a distinction between what was "really affirmed" (and this, in any event, was already an interpretation) and the way in which this affirmation was expressed—its "wording." But in those past times this *manner of presentation* was vital to the question of whether the statement concerning the faith was or was not true. Those Christians of the past could present the faith only in the way they did present it—*for them* the dogma stood or fell with the form in which *they* expressed it. Hence it is clear that in its historical situation the teaching authority of the Church could not but press for a specific *idea* or wording of the dogma, because in the intellectual climate of the time a denial of the manner of presentation of the dogma inevitably suggested a denial of the real article of faith it expressed. Indeed such a challenge to the manner of presentation very often did more than *suggest* a denial of doctrine: an inflexible disregard for the form of expression frequently meant a genuine denial of the real content of the dogma itself!

It is only after the passage of time has produced a different climate of thought that meaningful questions can be raised concerning the "wording" of the dogmatic definitions of the past; in other words, that the process of finding new interpretations faithful to these definitions can begin. As long as man's perspective and climate of thought have not changed, he will take over the dogma as a whole—that is, together with the framework within which he must necessarily think in order to experience the dogma meaningfully. No one can ever anticipate history, although all kinds of implicit tendencies betray—afterwards—that the future has been prepared in the past. When history has moved forward, texts from the past acquire a new fulfilment. Thus, every generation is able to study Plato or Augustine, for example, anew—the past lives again and again in a new way, and indeed in such a way that the distinctively Platonic and the distinctively Augustinian sense and meaning of their works is inwardly really fulfilled and not by way of "inegesis," but by faithful exegesis! In the same way, there can be no end to the interpretative rereading of the Bible. In every generation the Church rereads Holy Scripture, and she has been doing this for two thousand years, during which time the Bible has gradually been revealing its *own* meaning, thanks to the light in which the past comes to stand in the present. The same applies to conciliar texts. The fact that the biblical and conciliar statements convey a mystery does not eliminate the historical character of human thought and faith.

Therefore in examining, in faith, statements made in the past by the Church, we must take present problems into account. Otherwise we hardly need to examine these earlier statements at all—we shall know in advance what we shall find. It will be the dogma together with its historical framework of thought and wording, as this is reconstructed for us by the historian, and, as believers, we shall be precisely where we started! Bonaventure and Thomas "demythologised" the "profession of faith" Berengarius was obliged to sign in the light of their new Aristotelian way of thinking: in other words, they took it out of the "sensualistic" framework within which a Roman synod in the eleventh century had formulated the real presence of Christ in the Eucharist. Some epigons are clearly unable to show moderation, but this does not mean that by an appeal to the Council of Trent we should call a halt to the genuine effort being made at the moment throughout the whole world (and especially in Western Europe) to understand the real content of "transubstantiation." If we were to do this, we should perhaps (the possibility is *a priori* there) be invoking the authority not of a dogma but of an earlier way of thinking! The authority of the Church's pronouncements would be maintained against modernists, but the fact that we were only appealing to the earlier framework of thought would be lost to sight, whereas the so-called modernists are really deeply concerned with the problem of making the inviolable *dogma* itself once again relevant to the faithful of today by separating it from a framework of ideas within which faith can no longer thrive in the present age.

But this "separation" must be done with great care, because we are concerned here with a mystery we cannot lay hold of and grasp in our hands, as we can the earth, for example. What we have here is one of the most delicate of all the living mysteries of the Catholic faith which cannot be stripped of its splendour without causing great harm to the faithful.

The Text of the Dogma: Its Origin, Growth and Final Drafting

Before the Council of Trent, certain *theologi minores* (conciliar experts who were not bishops), with a view to making the discussions in the Council about the Eucharist easier, had studied Protestant publications and compiled a list of statements which, in their opinion, could not be accepted by a Catholic.[1] These statements were first examined by the assembled theologians.[2] The result of their work was then handed to the fathers of the Council, who used the text as a basis for their discussions and as a basis on which the Council (in the present case at least) would build up its dogmatic definition. The discussions in plenary congregation which began in Trent were interrupted by the threat of plague, and the Council was transferred for a time to Bologna. Later, they were resumed in Trent and brought to a conclusion.

[1] *Concilii Tridentini Acta,* ed. Goerres Gesellschaft, pt. 5, pp. 869–961; pt. 6, p. 123; pt. 7, pp. 111–43 (see pt. 1, pp. 608–9).
[2] *Ibid.,* pt. 1, p. 615; pt. 5, pp. 869–70, 960 ff., 1008; pt. 6, pp. 123 ff.

All that concerns us here, at least directly, is the genesis of canon 1 and canon 2.[3] The very first basic text of the statements which were condemned by canons 1 and 2, in the form in which it was distributed for discussion in the plenary congregation of February 1547, was as follows:

1. *"In the Eucharist, the body and blood of our Lord Jesus Christ is not truly (present), but as in a sign, just as it is said that there is wine in a signboard outside a tavern (a cup or some other symbol on a signboard at the entrance to a drinking house). That is the error of Zwingli, Oecolampadius and the Sacramentarians."*[4]

2. *(in fact 3 here) "In the Eucharist, the body and blood of our Lord Jesus Christ is truly (present), but at the same time with the substance of bread and wine, so that there is no transubstantiation, but a hypostatic union of (Christ's) humanity with the substance of bread and wine. For Luther says. . . ."*[5]

I shall, for the time being, not consider the question as to how far these theologians accurately reproduced the Reformers' views in these texts.

The first draft (first schema) of the two canons was made on the basis of these two theses and distributed to the Coun-

[3] Denzinger 883-4 (1651-2).

[4] *Concilii Tridentini Acta,* pt. 5, p. 869; to be condemned, see pt. 7, p. 142: see pt. 7, pp. 111-2 (of the 2nd of Sept., 1551, with a slightly changed text).

[5] *Ibid.;* also pt. 7, p. 112 (slightly changed). Also an affirmation to be condemned: pt. 7, p. 142.

cil fathers before the plenary discussions which began on the
9th of May, 1547:

   1. "*If anyone should maintain that the sacrament of the Eu-*
charist does not truly (re vera) *contain* (contineri in sacramento) *the body and blood of our Lord Jesus Christ, but (that*
these) are only there (ibi esse) *as in a sign or a symbolic form*
(in figura), *let him be excommunicated.*"[6]

   2. "*Should anyone maintain that the sacrament of the Eucharist*
contains the body and blood of our Lord Jesus Christ in a man-
ner which is different from that which the holy Catholic Church
has hitherto preached and taught, that is, by a unique and won-
derful changing of the whole substance of bread into the body
and of the whole substance of wine into the blood, so that, under
the two species and, in breaking or separation, in each particle
(or part), the whole Christ is contained, which change was very
suitably called (nuncupata est) *transubstantiation by our fathers,*[7]
let him be excommunicated."[8]

These texts were submitted to the fathers of the Council
for discussion. In the congregation of the 17th to the 23rd of
May, 1547, various *censurae,* or amendments, were suggested
by the fathers. Those which concern us here are the following. In canon 1, some of the fathers objected to *re vera,*

---

  [6] *Ibid.,* pt. 6, p. 124.

  [7] It is clear from other texts that the phrase "our fathers" here referred
to the Fathers of the Church and to the fathers of, among others, the
Fourth Lateran Council: *Concilii Tridentini Acta, op. cit.,* pt. 6, p. 156.

  [8] *Ibid.,* pt. 6, p. 124.

"truly," and preferred terms which were rather more em-
phatic—*vere et realiter, realiter et veraciter, substantialiter et
realiter* or *vere et substantialiter*.[9] In canon 2, the interpolation of the clause "while the species (*species*) of bread and
wine nonetheless remain"[10] was demanded, because no mention had been made of this in the official schema which had
been discussed (in contrast to various personal schemas,
which had not been debated). These amendments were examined on the 17th of May by a commission of *theologi
maiores* (theologians who were at the same time bishops).[11]
The formula *vere et realiter* was accepted.[12] In addition, the
word "contained in" (*contineri*) in the same canon 2 was
replaced by "is present" (*esse*). What is remarkable is that
some of the bishops (although they proved to be in a mi-
nority) objected to the word *praesentia* and preferred the
more objectivistic words *esse* or *contineri in*.[13]

An extremely interesting suggestion, put forward by
Bishop Th. Casellus in the conciliar debate and defended by
him in the commission (of which he was a member), was
rejected with one vote in favour (his own): "because of the
scholastics," as he said, he preferred to speak more precisely
of a "sacramental change" (*conversio sacramentalis*), instead
of the exuberant but rather meaningless adjectives "unique

[9] In the summary of the discussions: pt. 6, p. 142.

[10] Pt. 6, p. 136.

[11] Pt. 6, pp. 145–7.

[12] Pt. 6, p. 146.

[13] Pt. 6, pp. 134, 135 and 140, as against pp. 135, 136, 137, 138 and
140, where the word *praesentia* was agreed to.

and wonderful" in connection with the *conversio*.[14] From the sacramental theological point of view, I personally think that this was one of the best suggestions that was made during these sessions. It was, unfortunately, not taken up, and the acts of the Council do not tell us why. The bishop was clearly reacting against a "sensualistic" and crudely realistic view of the Eucharist, whereas the fathers of the Council never stressed those points on which Catholic and Protestant Christians were in agreement (in our case, the *sacramentality* of the *whole* eucharistic event), but only reacted against the Reformers in their canons.

The canons were consequently revised, and the second, amended schema was submitted to the plenary congregation for discussion on the 25th of May, 1547:

1. "If anyone should maintain that the most holy *sacrament of the Eucharist does not* truly and really (vere et realiter) *contain the body and blood of our Lord Jesus Christ, but only as in a sign or a symbolic form* (in figura), *let him be excommunicated.*"[15]

2. "Should anyone maintain that, in the sacrament of the Eucharist, the body and blood of our Lord Jesus Christ is (present) *in a manner which is different from that which the holy Catholic Church has hitherto* held, *that is, by a unique and wonderful changing of the whole substance of bread into the body and of the whole substance of wine into the blood,* while the species (species) of bread and wine nonetheless remain, *so that, under*

[14] Pt. 6, p. 139.
[15] Pt. 6, p. 155.

each part, the whole Christ is present (is contained), which
change was very suitably called transubstantiation by our fathers,
let him be excommunicated."[16]

The amended schema was examined by the plenary congregation on the 25th of May, 1547, and all kinds of new
amendments were suggested.[17] One remarkable suggestion
was that the word "species" (*species*) should be changed to
"accidents."[18] The commission of *theologi maiores* discussed
the new suggestions on the 27th of May. As the commission
could not decide whether to allow the word "species" to
stand or whether to replace it by "accidents," the matter
was put to the vote. The result was an equal number of votes
for each word, and the text (which was "in possession") remained unchanged.[19] The new text went back to the Council and the two basic canons at least (those with which we
are concerned here) were accepted without new corrections.
They were, however, not published.

For many different reasons, these texts on the Eucharist
were left untouched for about four years. It was not until
September 1551 that the question was taken up again (this
time, once more in Trent itself).[20] Although the canons
which were formulated at Bologna were taken as a point of

---

[16] Here and in the later amendments I have italicised additions that
were new in comparison with the preceding schema. Omissions will be
revealed by a comparison of the texts.

[17] Pt. 6, pp. 156–9, with the summary pp. 159–60.

[18] Pt. 6, pp. 157 and 159. (See also pt. 7, p. 185: "quae per se
subsistere possit.")

[19] Pt. 6, pp. 160–1.   [20] Pt. 7, pp. 110–204.

departure,[21] everything would seem to point to the fact that the whole question was fundamentally re-examined. On the basis of the previous theses, the theologians drew up a number of theses taken from the works of Protestant writers. The two which had been the basis of the two dogmatic "canons" remained in fundamentally the same form (as mentioned above).[22] These theses were, at least as far as their content was concerned, again taken as a basis for the two later canons (which express in the form of an anathema what the Protestant affirmations assert positively), after having first been discussed both by the theologians[23] and by the bishops.[24] As far as our two canons are concerned, only a few new elements appeared. Bishop Martin Ayala (of Guadix in Spain) asked that "and not only by its saving efficacy" (*in virtute*)[25] should be interpolated in canon i after "not only as in a sign." This was not, as has often been said, aimed at Calvin (who was never named in connection with transubstantiation), but was inserted simply "in order more clearly to condemn the position of the heretics." In the case of the Eucharist, it was clearly not even sufficient

[21] Pt. 7, p. 177.

[22] Pt. 7, pp. 111–2. Only the first "thesis" (*articulus*) was made more concise and matter-of-fact and was given a new interpolation: "In the Eucharist, neither the body and blood *nor the divinity* of our Lord Jesus Christ is truly (present), but only as in sign. This is the error of Zwingli, Oecolampadius and the Sacramentarians" (*ibid.*, p. 111). This should be compared with the previous text (see above, footnote 4 of the present chapter).

[23] Pt. 7, pp. 111–43.

[24] Pt. 7, pp. 143–76.

[25] Pt. 7, p. 162.

to say that it was a *signum efficax,* an effective sign of salvation. The amended canons, which were distributed on the 3rd of October, 1551, were as follows:

1. "If anyone should maintain that the most holy sacrament of the Eucharist does not truly, really and substantially *contain the body and blood* together with the soul and divinity *of our Lord Jesus Christ and* thus the whole Christ, *but (that these) are only there (present) as in a sign or figure* or (only) by efficacity, *let him be excommunicated."*

2. (in fact 3 in this text) "Should anyone maintain that, in the most holy *sacrament of the Eucharist,* the substance of bread and wine remains (in existence) together with the body and blood of our Lord Jesus Christ *or that,* according to detestable and profane modernist words (vocum novitates), Christ is "impanated" *(united with the remaining substance of bread)* and should deny this *wonderful and unique changing of the whole substance of bread into the body and of the whole substance of wine into the blood, while the species of bread and wine nonetheless remain, which change our fathers and* the universal Catholic Church *have very suitably called transubstantiation, let him be excommunicated."*[26]

The list of adverbs, "truly, really and substantially"— *vere, realiter* and *substantialiter* (see the earlier texts)—only gave greater emphasis to the original *re vera,* "authentically real," the aim being to eliminate any possibility that the meaning might be reduced. The word "substantially," how-

[26] Pt. 7, p. 178.

ever, has a special shade of meaning that I shall explain later.

A discussion of these new canons reveals a number of interesting facts (some of which will not be considered until the second chapter of this book). For example, a bishop suggested that, in the expression "truly present," the distinctively sacramental character of the eucharistic presence should be stressed by inserting the words "really and sacramentally"[27] and by leaving out "by efficacy," because Christ is also present *in virtute* in the Eucharist.[28] The text about the "impanated Christ" was also criticised by the fathers of the Council, who said that no Protestant had ever made such an assertion.[29] It was only at this stage too (a few days before the declaration of the dogma) that the idea of preceding the negative, condemnatory canons by a concise, positive exposition of Catholic teaching was brought up.[30] The text that was amended by the commission (the schema of the 9th of October, 1551, which was in fact, as far as canons 1 and 2 are concerned, exactly the same as the definitive text of the dogma; see later) was as follows:

1. "If anyone should deny *that the most holy sacrament of the Eucharist truly, really and substantially contains the body and*

[27] Pt. 7, p. 183: "realiter et sacramentaliter."

[28] Pt. 7, pp. 183, 184 and (three interventions) p. 185.

[29] Pt. 7, p. 182 (twice), p. 183 and p. 184.

[30] The so-called *capita:* pt. 7, pp. 177 and 185. Mgr. A. Foscararius (Modena) and Mgr. A. Ayala (Guadix, Spain) were given the task of formulating these *capita* (pt. 7, p. 188), which were revised by the working commission. See the definitive text: Denzinger 873a–882 (1635–50).

*blood together with the soul and divinity of our Lord Jesus Christ
and thus the whole Christ, but should say that they (body, blood,
etc.) are only (present) as in a sign or figure or (only) by
(their) efficacy, let him be excommunicated."*

2. *"Should anyone maintain that, in the most holy sacrament
of the Eucharist, the substance of bread and wine remains (in
existence) together with the body and blood of our Lord Jesus
Christ and should deny this wonderful and unique changing of
the whole substance of bread into the body and of the whole
substance of wine into the blood, while the species of bread and
wine nonetheless remain, which change* the Catholic Church *very
suitably* calls *transubstantiation, let him be excommunicated."*[31]

The changes were therefore very slight. What is striking
is that the historical relativity of the Church's use of the
word "transubstantiation" was acknowledged. Whereas
there had previously been an inclination to regard the use
of the term, despite some protests, at least materially as
scriptural, patristic and conciliar custom and even to attribute it to the *universal* Church (as the previous schemas had
done—"our fathers and the universal Catholic Church"),
there was a sudden change in this schema, which did not
refer to the past and simply stated "the Catholic Church"
(leaving out the word "universal") very suitably calls (that
is, *now* in any case) "transubstantiation." The bishops—
more were present at the Council in 1551 than in 1547 and
more too from outside Italy—had strongly criticised this

[31] Pt. 7, p. 187.

generalised and, from the historical point of view, basically incorrect assertion.[32] The theory of an "impanation," regarded as a kind of extension of the "hypostatic union," was also omitted completely because, as one bishop maintained, no Protestant had ever expressed such an opinion.[33]

The new canons were once again submitted to the Council for discussion and the amendments were dealt with by a commission. Apart from the transposition of two small words for the sake of style, there were no changes in the two canons which concern us here. This schema was therefore at the same time the definitive and dogmatic text, which was solemnly approved on the 11th of October, 1551.[34]

Some Hermeneutic Afterthoughts

The basic intention of the fathers of the Council was made clear in *cap.* 4 of the "Decree on the most holy sacrament of the Eucharist," a commentary on canon 2—it was *precisely because* Christ understood the handing over of his body under the form of bread in a very real sense that the Church's conviction (which this synod wishes to proclaim explicitly now) has *therefore* always been that the entire

[32] See especially pt. 7, p. 183 and (three interventions) p. 184, also p. 125.

[33] "Non est error temporis praesentis" (pt. 7, p. 163; see also pt. 7, pp. 183 and 184).

[34] Pt. 7, the *capita* pp. 200–3 and the canons pp. 203–4. See also Denzinger 883 and 884 (1651–2).

substance of the bread is changed into the body of Christ our Lord and the entire substance of the wine is changed into the substance of his blood by the consecration of bread and wine. This change was, in a suitable and appropriate manner, called transubstantiation by the holy Catholic Church.[35] As a result of this, canon 2 goes on to say, the substance of bread and wine is no longer present after the consecration—the really present reality is the body and blood of Christ, the entire concrete Christ (in his divinity and in his humanity), "while the species of bread and wine nonetheless remain." This happens by virtue of a change which the Church very suitably calls transubstantiation.

It is clear from the acts of the Council that there was no discussion at all about the concept "change" (*conversio*)—this was accepted by everyone without further ado. There was some doubt, however, about whether the term "transubstantiation" should also be insisted upon. The expression had, after all, only a short tradition behind it, and one father of the Council, apparently counting centuries as years, even went so far as to claim: "Say rather that the Church has been making use of this word for a few years."[36] It was therefore not primarily a question of the word or the expression "transubstantiation." Certain bishops even asked for this word to be suppressed, believing that a council

[35] Denzinger 877 (1642). The past tense, "was called," is preserved in the *caput*. These *capita* were, however, not discussed in detail by the Council itself and, unlike the canons, they have no precise dogmatic value. They form, as it were, an explanatory *nota praevia*, although of a rather more official kind.

[36] *Concilii Tridentini Acta, op. cit.*, pt. 7, p. 184.

ought not to take over such a (recently introduced) current term.[37]

On the other hand, many of the Council fathers pointed to the new word *homoousios,* "consubstantial" ("homoousian," of the same nature or substance), which also did not occur in Scripture, but which the earlier Fathers of the Church seemed to have found necessary in order to expose christological heresies.[38] Divergent views about faith, in other words, made it necessary to use new words. The term was consequently accepted, especially since it had been explicitly and firmly rejected by Luther.[39] In other words, like the word "homoousian" previously, the term "transubstantiation" was, for the Council of Trent, a political banner of the orthodox faith, very suitably proclaiming, in the sixteenth-century situation, the difference between the Reformers' and the Catholic view of the Eucharist. As such, the word itself explained nothing. It was simply intended as a kind of distinguishing mark by which the Christian could make his own position in the doctrine of the Eucharist immediately clear. It has lost this significance in our own times—even Protestant theologians have discovered and accepted the suggestive force of the word "transubstantiation." It has lost its function as a banner because it can now be used to fly over ships with different cargoes.

[37] Pt. 7, p. 188 (see also pp. 182 and 125).

[38] For example, pt. 5, p. 944. In the debate of 1551, this argument was constantly occurring: pt. 7, pp. 114–86; especially in the case of Melchior Cano: pt. 7, p. 125.

[39] Pt. 5, p. 188; pt. 7, p. 112.

The fathers of the Council of Trent set out with much more important questions in mind than simply this terminology, the relative value of which is clearly displayed in the final statement, "it is a very suitable term." No more was claimed for it than this. What is more, the Bishop of Vienna even asked, fully three days before the dogma was solemnly published, for the term "transubstantiation" to be omitted![40] What, then, was basically at stake? The Council wanted to safeguard the significance of the "real presence" of the Eucharist within the Church. Zwingli, Oecolampadius and the Sacramentarians had exclusively emphasised the symbolic significance. The Catholic Church had always proclaimed the sacramental species of the Eucharist to be "signs," and the Council of Trent had nothing to say against this. Canon 1 therefore only condemned the thesis according to which the eucharistic presence was interpreted "exclusively and only" (*tantummodo*) as a sacramental symbolism, as is, for example, the case with baptism and the other sacraments.

Furthermore, the Council said, it was not sufficient to regard this eucharistic presence as being of the same order as Christ's presence in the other sacraments, because he was really persent "by efficacy" in those sacraments; that is, Christ's personal act of giving himself acquired, in the sign of the sacramental symbolic action of, for example, baptism, a visible form for anyone who received the sacrament. In baptism there was therefore a real giving of himself on the part of Christ in a symbolic act. But in this interpretation,

[40] Pt. 7, p. 188.

the distinctive quality of Christ's presence in the Eucharist was not guaranteed. Something more profound was accomplished in it. The Council did not say, therefore, that there was a real presence of Christ only in the Eucharist. It was not until the time of Scotus that the real presence of Christ was identified for the first time with his specific presence in the Eucharist—and this was unfortunate, for is not Christ also really present (non-eucharistically) in the service of the word and in the assembled community of believers (as explicitly professed in the Second Vatican Council's Constitution on the Liturgy, c. I, n. 7)? But Christ's real presence in the Eucharist is something else.

Each of these different forms of Christ's single real presence has its own distinctive mode of reality. But the Council of Trent had the task of defending and professing the distinctive mode of Christ's real presence *in the Eucharist*. That was the Council's basic intention, and it is in the light of this that the canons must be read and interpreted. (To constitute a real synthesis, any review of this presence—that is, Christ's real presence in the Eucharist—should involve, at the same time, a consideration of this eucharistic presence against the background of Christ's real presence in the entire liturgy. This real presence in the whole liturgy includes not only Christ's presence in the liturgical proclamation of the word, but also his real presence in the community of believers gathered for the celebration of the Eucharist. But unfortunately, as I have already said, this background must be assumed here without further exposition. I take this course reluctantly, with the aim of concentrating attention on the one point—Christ's real presence in the Eucharist.)

We are at once aware of three different levels in the Tridentine dogma:

1. At the very centre of the dogma is the Tridentine affirmation of a specific and distinctive *eucharistic* presence—namely, the real presence of Christ's body and blood under the sacramental species of bread and wine—a presence which is understood in so deep and real a sense that Jesus was able to say: This here, this is my body; I hand it over to you for you to eat, so that you may have communion with me. For this reason, Christ is "truly, really and substantially" present, and not *only* present "as in a sign" or "by efficacity" (canon 1) or simply at communion, but also before (after the liturgy of the consecration) and afterwards. The insistence of the Tridentine dogma on the *lasting* character of Christ's real presence in the Eucharist points to the special and distinctive reality of this particular presence.[41]

2. The Council of Trent was unable to express this eucharistic real presence in any other way than on the basis of a change of the substance of bread and wine into the substance of Christ's body and blood (canon 2).

3. This change of bread and wine was very suitably called transubstantiation (the concluding sentence of canon 2).

I have already discussed this third and fairly relative level; in other words, the question of terminology. The question which immediately presents itself now is, What is the re-

[41] Denzinger 886 (1654), although *cap.* 5 says explicitly that this presence ultimately continues to be directed towards sacramental communion: "ut sumatur institutum" (Denzinger 878 [1643]).

lationship between the first and the second levels, between the first and the second canons? Are they two different dogmas? The introductory *cap.* 4 clearly establishes the connection: *because* there is a specifically eucharistic real presence, there must *therefore* be a "change of the one substance into the other." This emerges even more clearly from the previous stage(s) of canon 2: "should anyone maintain that, in the sacrament of the Eucharist, the body and blood of our Lord Jesus Christ is (present) *in a manner which is different* from that which the holy Catholic Church has hitherto held, that is, by a changing . . . etc."[42] The Council was clearly concerned with the distinctive character of the real presence of Christ in the Eucharist—with no more than this, but also with no less than this. This was very suggestively illustrated by the interventions on the part of various bishops, some of whom expressed the opinion that what the Council wanted to express positively as a change of substance by the term transubstantiation had already been said in as many words in the first statement, namely, that Christ

---

[42] See above, footnote 8 (pt. 6, p. 124), also footnote 15 (pt. 6, p. 155), referring to the second schema of the canon. The same is clear from Seripando's personal draft. (The first offical draft was based on Seripando's preliminary study.) Seripando's words were: "If anyone should maintain that the body and blood of Christ are present in the Eucharist *in any other manner* than in the manner which the Church . . . etc." (pt. 6, p. 131). The statement of Mgr. Musso, the Bishop of Bitonto and the official defender of the text in its final stage, was especially strongly worded, namely, canon 1 says how transubstantiation is ("quomodo sit transsubstantiatio") and canon 2 says how transubstantiation comes about ("quomodo fiat sit transsubstantiatio"), pt. 7, p. 188. The eucharistic *praesentia realis* therefore *is* transubstantiation.

was "truly, really and substantially" present in the Eucharist.

This view was expressed particularly in the session of 1551. No separate justification was provided for the error of canon 2, for many bishops maintained that the opposite was apparent from the falsehood of the first thesis (canon 1).[43] The second canon was only a different formulation of what had already been said in the first canon. In other words, the canon dealing with transubstantiation added nothing new, as far as its *content* was concerned, to the canon dealing with the specifically and distinctively real presence in the Eucharist. Eucharistic "real presence" and "transubstantiation" were, in the minds of the fathers of the Council, identical as affirmations. But, despite this identity, Melchior Cano especially pointed out at the Council that the new formulation did not therefore belong to faith in quite the same way as the first statement did. This theologian—who had, in his time, been particularly concerned with the method of theol-

---

[43] Again and again we find the phrase repeated: "(art. 2, here still art. 3) continetur in primo" or "(art. 2) haereticus est ex primo," as, for example, in pt. 7, p. 149, p. 158, p. 161, p. 165 and (twice) p. 170. As far as I know, there was only one father who did not clearly see the relationship and asked for the second canon to come first (pt. 7, p. 183), apparently reasoning that transubstantiation was there "first" and the eucharistic presence then came about because of it. The Council itself, on the other hand, reasoned the other way about—starting from the biblical affirmation of the eucharistic real presence. It would similarly be wrong to claim that some of the fathers of the Council wanted to delete the second canon (as implied in the first). (Some authors have obviously been caught by the fact that, in some stages of the discussions, our "canon 2" became "canon 3," because an entirely different canon was inserted as "canon 2" between our two canons.)

ogy—appeared, in other words, to *sense* that it was possible
to give orthodox affirmation to the content of the first canon
while at the same time remaining sceptical about the *formulation* of the second.[44]

If we look at this historical result with the modern problem in mind, we at once see the red light—the fathers of the
Council of Trent could not establish or express the real
presence of Christ in the Eucharist unless they insisted on
the acceptance of a transubstantiation of bread and wine.
But, in that case, the theologian is immediately confronted
with the question, Is this necessary connection between the
"real presence" in the Eucharist and "transubstantiation" an
inner necessity of the dogma itself or is it something that was
necessary, in the spiritual and intellectual climate of the age,
to thought—the only way in which the dogma of the eucharistic real presence could, *at that time,* readily be established?
If the latter is the case, then the affirmation of a "change of
substances" was no more than a formal repetition of the
eucharistic "real presence"—in other words, different logical
terms were being used in the second canon to say the same,
as far as the content was concerned, as had been said in the
first. The solution to this problem is vital to the question
as to whether the Tridentine dogma of the real presence
of Christ in the Eucharist displays an aspect of "wording,"
to which the Church, then, is not bound for all time, or
whether it does not in fact display this aspect. To judge
from the various drafts of the definitive canon 2, from the
purport of *cap.* 4 and from the interventions on the part of

[44] Pt. 7, p. 125.

several of the fathers of the Council, it is in any case quite clear that the fathers were really concerned with the unique and distinctive (Catholic) quality of the real presence of Christ in the Eucharist. But it is also clear that these fathers were firmly convinced that they could not safeguard this distinctively eucharistic presence of Christ unless they also insisted on the acceptance of a "change of substances." What has obviously emerged, then, is that the final statement was without doubt secondary and that it was there purely to explicitate the first statement in a polemical context.

On the other hand, however, despite the fact that many bishops claimed that canons 1 and 2 were, as far as their contents were concerned, identical, the Council ultimately devoted a separate canon to the second affirmation—that is, to transubstantiation. From one point of view at least, it is even possible to say that the Council of Trent placed the emphasis on the second affirmation—*because* there is a specifically eucharistic real presence, the Council *therefore* insists on transubstantiation (*cap.* 4). We can therefore, and indeed must, say that the Council was pointing directly towards transubstantiation, *because* the *real* intention was to safeguard the eucharistic real presence—as *cap.* 4 says, "quoniam . . . ideo. . . ." This means, in other words, that the Council of Trent was unable to express this unique presence in any other way but on the basis of a transubstantiation. Anyone denying this transubstantiation would at the same time be denying this particular presence, and this was what was at stake in the Catholic faith.

Both Bonaventure and Thomas, for example, presented it

in the same way. They took as their point of departure the distinctive quality of the sacramental presence of Christ's body and blood—that was the biblical datum, the dogma and therefore the norm for their speculation about this aspect of faith. From this point of departure, they came to a "theological conclusion"—*because* a presence *of this kind* cannot come about unless it does so by means of a change of the reality of the bread into the reality of Christ's body, we must *therefore* accept transubstantiation.[45] Both Bonaventure and Thomas began with the indisputable fact of faith— here is a distinctive real presence.[46] Because of what this inevitably implied for them, they spoke, in the *second* place —that is, on the basis of theological reasoning—of a change of the substance of the bread. In comparison with the first dogmatic statement of *faith,* their affirmation of this change of substance is a *theologoumenon,* despite the fact that, even

[45] Thomas, *ST, III*, q. 75, a. 4 (transubstantiation) *after* a. 1 (eucharistic real presence). Bonaventure, *In IV Sent,.* d. 11, pars 1, art. unicus, q. 1-q. 6: pp. 241-53 (*de transsubstantiatione*) *after* d. 10: pp. 216-38 (on the real presence).

[46] A presence that is difficult to define: "quodam speciali modo, qui est proprius huic sacramento" (Thomas, *ST, III*, q. 75, a. 1, ad 3). As a non-local presence, it is a *spiritual* presence of Christ's true body, born of the Virgin Mary and risen from the dead. The term *praesentia realis* (as applied to and characteristic of the Eucharist) was not known in the thirteenth century. Thomas himself used many different expressions—a "praesentia corporis Christi" (*ST, III*, q. 75, a. 1, ad 4), "spiritualiter" (*ibid.*), "esse in hoc sacramento" (*ST, III*, q. 75, a. 1), "hoc sacramentum ipsum Christum realiter continet . . . secundum rei veritatem" (*ibid.*), "veritas corporis et sanguinis Christi" (*ibid*), "invisibiliter" (*ibid.*), "non in propria specie, sed sub speciebus huius sacramenti" (*ibid.*, ad 2), "esse sub sacramento" (*ST, III*, q. 76, a. 6), etc.

before the time of Bonaventure and Thomas, certain Roman synods had already spoken about *substantialiter converti*.[47] Innocent III had referred to *transsubstantiari* in 1202[48] and the Fourth Lateran Council had used the term *transsubstantiatio*.[49] In this context at least, Thomas did not even refer to these texts. For him, it was first and foremost something that was necessary to thought—this distinctively eucharistic real presence could not be established in any other way but by proposing a change of the substance of the bread.[50] It was also precisely the same for Bonaventure, but, *in addition* to regarding this as necessary to thought (the opposite being *contrarium rationi*), he was *also* to appeal to the universal tradition of the Church.[51] For Thomas especially, the

[47] See footnote 8 of the introduction.

[48] Denzinger 416 (784).

[49] Denzinger 430 (802).

[50] " . . . et propter hoc relinquitur quod *non possit aliter corpus* Christi incipere esse de novo in hoc sacramento *nisi per* conversionem substantiae panis in ipsum" (Thomas, *ST*, III, q. 75, a. 2).

[51] "*Communiter* tenet ecclesia quod est ibi conversio" (Bonaventure, *In IV Sent.*, d. 11, pars 1, art. unicus, q. 1: pt. 4, p. 242 B, 243 B; and q. 3: p. 246 B). Thomas certainly referred to the condemnation of Berengarius in connection with the latter's *praesentia corporalis* (*ST*, III, q. 75, a. 1) and in connection with his affirmation that the *substantia panis,* in his opinion, remained after the consecration (*ST*, III, q. 75, a. 2). But, whereas, in the first case, he referred to the fact that the Church obliged Berengarius to retract his statement, he did not, in the second case (a. 2) make use of argument based on the authority of the Church, but only of purely rational argument. He recognised more clearly than Bonaventure the difference "in level" between the affirmation of the eucharistic presence (which was, for him, a datum of faith) and the "change of the substance" (which was, for him, a cogent theological conclusion).

"change of the substance" of the bread and the wine was a theological conclusion drawn *from* the datum of faith of the unique eucharistic presence. It was only then—in the *third* place, as it were—that Thomas appealed to the Aristotelian doctrine of the substance and its accidents.[52]

The whole affair, then, was full of subtle distinctions in the entire tradition that preceded the Council of Trent. A clear distinction was above all made between the real datum of *faith,* which was, in the last resort, biblical,[53] and the way in which this datum was expressed and interpreted. As we have already seen, some of those who were present at the Council sensed this difference in level. There was, however, this important distinction—the Council of Trent was an "ecumenical council" testifying here, on the basis of its supreme authority, to the fact that it could not uphold the biblical affirmation of faith in its purity without at the same time affirming the change of the substance of the bread and the wine. In such circumstances, too, it is important to take into account the difference between a *"theological* development" of the doctrine and a "development of *dogma."* In

[52] In *ST,* III, q. 77, after having spoken, in q. 75-6, about the eucharistic presence and then, after this, about the "change of the substance" of the bread.

[53] See, in addition to the well-known technical and exegetical studies, the excellent synthesis provided by J. Betz in *Die Eucharistie in der Zeit der griechischen Väter,* Pt. II-1, *Die Realpräsenz des Leibes und Blutes Jesu im Abendmahl nach dem Neuen Testament,* Freiburg i. Br., second enlarged edition (1965). A concise but careful study of the *praesentia realis* in Paul and John has been provided by B. van Iersel, "De 'praesentia realis' in het Nieuwe Testament," *Praesentia realis,* Nijmegen (1963), pp. 7-18 (*Sanct. Euch.* 55 [1963], July and August).

other words, something that has once been recognised in theology simply as a theological conclusion may, at a later stage, be affirmed by the mind of the whole Church and ultimately even by the official charism of the Church's teaching authority as a true datum of *faith*. We have therefore not yet finished with the simple assertion that there were at the Council of Trent statements at two different levels of not quite equal value.

In the light of the report on the Protestant assertions made by the conciliar theologians and submitted to the fathers of the Council, the first canon (the one dealing with Christ's real presence in the Eucharist) was clearly directed against Zwingli, Oecolampadius and the Sacramentarians, who appeared to misrepresent the unique and distinctive character of the eucharistic presence. Neither Luther nor Calvin was mentioned in this connection. The Tridentine theologians had a distinct feeling for what was Catholic in Luther's view of the eucharistic presence. On the other hand, they were also aware of a fundamental difference between Luther's total view and the Catholic view—Luther accepted this unique presence only during the liturgy and therefore at communion (only *in usu*) and was sharply opposed to the Roman practice of "reserving" the sacrament. This could at least possibly have indicated a different view of the real presence in the Eucharist, a view which seemed to be expressed in Luther's opinion that the bread remained simply bread after the consecration. It was this that made his theory of "companation" (his theory that Christ and the bread co-existed) suspect, and it was for this reason that the second canon about the "change in the substance" of the bread was added, as a polemical move against Luther, who had, moreover, violently attacked the term "transubstantiation."

This shows once more that the fathers of the Council of Trent were really concerned with no more and no less than the pure question of *faith* in the real presence of Christ in the Eucharist. We can hardly, of course, ask how the Council would have reacted to a possible argument on the part of one of its theologians reasoning from a completely different frame of thinking and maintaining that there might well be other possible ways of thinking about and interpreting meaningfully this "true, real and substantial" presence of Christ's body and blood in the Eucharist. No such different point of view or way of thinking existed among Catholics in the sixteenth century, and none of the Tridentine theologians could have thought and reasoned in advance of his own time. All that we can do now, reflecting about the Tridentine doctrine, is to repeat that the *only* aim of the Council of Trent was to proclaim the unique and distinctive character of the eucharistic presence as an inviolable datum of faith.

The Concept "Substance," the Tradition of the Church and the Aristotelian Doctrine of Substance and Accidents

It is, however, quite possible that the second statement made by the Council of Trent (canon 2, on "transubstantiation") also contained two different levels. These may be formulated as follows. In the first place, the Council wished to affirm a *conversio* in the radical sense of the word and expressed this by the statement of a "change of substance." The second level is that of the Aristotelian doctrine of substance and accidents. So far, we have not yet established whether these two levels are in fact present or not in canon 2, and this is clearly what we must do now.

Generally speaking, most modern historians of the Council of Trent maintain that this Council completely dissociated itself from the Aristotelian philosophy of nature, claiming that this is especially evident from the deliberate avoidance of the word "accidents" and the use of the word *species* (or "forms"). Although I do agree that the fact, also put forward by these writers, that the Council stated in at least five different places that it only wished to make a stand against the Reformation and had no intention of settling scholastic disputes between Catholic theologians is undoubtedly correct,[54] I believe that the view that the Council deliberately avoided using the word "accidents" is historically incorrect and lacking in discernment. It is true, of course, that the word "accidents" was never used in any of the *official* Tridentine schemas. But it was used in unofficial texts which formed the basis for the official schemas. An example of this

---

[54] See *Concilii Tridentini Acta, op. cit.*, pt. 7, p. 189. Mgr. Cornelio Musso, the Bishop of Bitonto, who was appointed to defend the editing of the canons, said this explicitly. It was also a general attitude on the part of the whole Council, by order of Cardinal Crescentius, the first president of the Council and a papal legate.

is Seripando's schema, in which it was explicitly stated: "(change in the substance of bread and wine), while the accidents continue to exist without subject."[55] In the final sessions on the Eucharist a bishop suggested that the word "species" should be changed to "accidents" (see above). The commission which had to study the amendments submitted under Cardinal Cervini decided not to change the text because, as we have seen, there was an equal number of votes for each word.[56] The word *species* ("forms") consequently remained, and the justification for this decision is significant—the term *species* had a firm tradition behind it, and it had already been used by the Fourth Lateran Council, by the Council of Florence and by many theologians.[57] The other four voters said "utraque lectio placet" (*ibid.*)—in other words that both terms were equally good. The practical result was that the word "species" was retained because the text was juridically already "in possession." There is no mention in the whole of this discussion of any criticism of the word "accidents" as an Aristotelian term. The fathers of the Council of Trent were not trying to dissociate themselves from the word "accidents" for the very good reason that, whether they were strict Thomists or Scotists or whatever they were, they were all in their own way Aristotelian scholastics in their manner of thinking, and for all of them

[55] *Ibid.*, pt. 6, p. 131.

[56] See above, under footnotes 18 and 19 of this chapter.

[57] *Concilii Tridentini Acta, op. cit.,* pt. 6, pp. 160-1. The Fourth Lateran Council: Denzinger, 424 (793); see 414 (782); *Decretum pro Armenis* (Council of Florence): Denzinger, 698 (1321) (see the Second Council of Lyons: Denzinger, 465 [860]).

the words "species" (*species*) and "accidents" (*accidentia*) meant exactly the same in their *thinking* about faith and within the framework of faith.

This is precisely where so many of the historians of the Council of Trent go wrong—they are obstinate in their belief that the fathers wanted in one way or another to dissociate themselves from the Aristotelian manner of thinking. In this they are producing an anachronism and committing a hermeneutical blunder, which incidentally makes the modern reinterpretation of the dogma all the more difficult. As we have said, no single man, situated at a definite point in the history of the evolution of human thought, can be expected to dissociate himself from his own way of thinking (for him, an integral part of himself) and anticipate this history—in this case, to think some four centuries ahead! Although there were individual differences, the Aristotelian doctrine of substance and accidents formed the framework within which all the fathers of the Council of Trent thought. In reflecting about the datum of faith (of the unique real presence of Christ in the Eucharist), in considering it, not as a puzzle or a magic formula, but as a mystery of faith, they were bound to do so within their Aristotelian frame of reference. How could they have thought in any other way? Putting a distance between themselves and this way of thinking would, for them, have been equivalent to a refusal to think at all meaningfully about this mystery of faith! It is moreover historically unfair to see a "break" in the fathers' thinking about faith in the earlier conciliar texts in order to make it easier for us to think about these texts now in a new way. These modern authors believe that their theory facilitates reinterpretation of the Tridentine dogma, but in fact it only makes it more difficult! For, only if it becomes clear historically that the Tridentine dogma, without in fact sanctioning a particular philosophy, certainly expressed the datum of faith in Aristotelian terms will it be evident to the theologian (reasoning from the present stage of philosophical thought) that the dogma is bound to contain an aspect of "wording" which is historically determined and therefore unmistakably relative.

Some scholars have attempted to find out (in isolation from the modern problem and from their own manner of thinking about faith) precisely what the fathers of the Council of Trent believed and taught in connection with the Eucharist. To do this, they have tried to make a "reconstruction" excluding the older, then essential, ways of thinking. But a true interpretation of Trent is only possible—*objectively*—if both our own contemporary way of thinking and that of the fathers of the Council are brought to bear on the problem. This will be made clearer later on.

There is a great deal of evidence to show that there was not one of the fathers of the Council who did not think of the dogma in Aristotelian terms. There was certainly a feeling—ultimately biblical—that what was at stake was the distinctively *Catholic* character of the eucharistic presence; but, in order to insist on this distinctively Catholic quality, the fathers could not but express everything in contemporary terms (that is, in Aristotelian scholastic terms) *insofar* as it was necessary to do so in order to safeguard the dogma.

They were certainly aware of the difference between philosophy and faith, but they inevitably thought about faith in the concepts and categories, and within the whole framework, of their own thought. This does not imply any sanctioning by the Church of an Aristotelian philosophy; nonetheless, the whole Aristotelian doctrine of substance and accidents was the *framework of thought* within which the fathers of the Council reflected about faith. If it was ever to emerge, from the philosophical point of view, that the Aristotelian doctrine of substance and accidents was no longer tenable, there would be no reason for the dogma itself to suffer in any way. The Aristotelianism applied by Catholic theologians to the Eucharist was, after all, a radical "transubstantiation" of the authentic, historical Aristotelianism, which would never have tolerated any such division between substance and accidents! This insight certainly brings us one step closer to a solution of the problem.

Long before the Council of Trent, John Wycliffe (1320–84) wrote a book, *De eucharistia tractatus maior,*[58] in which, with reference to the real presence in the Eucharist, he quoted "three views" current in the Middle Ages—those of Thomas, Scotus and Berengarius.[59] He himself favoured the symbolic interpretation of Berengarius, and his justification of this is interesting. Wycliffe was an Aristotelian at Oxford University. Faithful to the authentic, historical Aristotelianism which could not admit any division between substance and accidents, he denied transubstantiation and

[58] Ed. J. Loserth, London (1892).
[59] *Ibid.,* pp. 29–30.

consequently, at that time, he also denied the specifically
Catholic view of the real presence in the Eucharist. Any
division between substance and accidents, Wycliffe maintained, was metaphysically impossible. His refusal to think
of the eucharistic presence in these Aristotelian categories
meant, within the *same* framework of thought, that Wycliffe could see no other way out of the difficulty than to
understand this presence purely symbolically, and this further implied that he was bound to formulate the eucharistic
presence thus conceived in Aristotelian terms as follows:
(1) the substance of bread and wine remains; (2) the accidents of bread and wine do not continue to exist without
subject; (3) there is consequently no "corporeal presence"
(*praesentia corporalis*) of Christ.[60]

This Aristotelian expression of a real presence not conceived in accordance with Catholic ideas forms the exact
obverse of the Tridentine formulation, which expressed the
Catholic view of the eucharistic presence in broadened Aristotelian terms. This clearly confirms what I have already
said about Trent—within the Aristotelian framework of
thought that prevailed in the Middle Ages, it was impossible
to safeguard the distinctively Catholic character of Christ's
real presence in the Eucharist without affirming transubstantiation. The fact that Wycliffe regarded himself as
obliged, on the basis of authentic Aristotelianism, to deny
transubstantiation led him inevitably to deny the dogma
of faith of the real presence in the Eucharist. Once again,

---

[60] See Wycliffe's condemnation by the Council of Constance (Denzinger,
n. 581–3 [1151–3]).

then, we may say that the concept "transubstantiation" points to nothing more, but also to nothing less, than the Catholic feeling for the biblical and distinctively eucharistic real presence of Christ within the medieval framework of thought.

At the Council of Constance, the Church condemned Wycliffe because of his purely symbolic interpretation of the eucharistic presence (Berengarius). But this condemnation was also inevitably expressed in the Aristotelian terms in which both Wycliffe and the Church thought at the time. The Council therefore condemned Wycliffe's thesis that the accidents of bread and wine did not continue to exist without subject after the consecration. This shows even more clearly than in Trent the correlation between the eucharistic presence and the Aristotelian view of substance and accidents. In the Middle Ages, this correlation was decisive to any view—either Catholic or non-Catholic—of the eucharistic presence.

The matter does not, however, end there. Although Trent was in fact much more sober in its Aristotelianism than the Council of Constance, it is true to say that all the fathers of the Council of Trent had the more pronounced Aristotelian formulae of Constance in mind when they condemned the Reformers' view of the eucharistic presence. The influence of the Council of Constance on that of Trent has been analysed by E. Gutwenger, who has, however, quite incorrectly inferred from this that Trent indirectly sanctioned the Aristotelian doctrine of substance and accidents as an inevitable ontological implication of the Catholic view of

the eucharistic presence.[61] It is certainly true that, in connection with the change of the substance of bread and wine,
the fathers and the theologians of the Council of Trent
made constant reference to the Council of Constance.[62]
Seripando's own preliminary study, which was an important
source for the final text, was virtually composed of formulae
from Constance.[63]

Finally, Trent also took up the condemnation of Wycliffe's three points again, but did it, as far as the Aristotelian
mode of expression was concerned, rather more soberly—
although the fathers of the Council of Trent still continued
to think about faith within the framework of Aristotelian
thought, they were at least more existentially sensitive to the
difference between philosophy and faith. That is why the
doctrine of substance and accidents was, both for Constance
and for Trent, more than simply a question of "wording."
The fathers of the Council of Trent were not explicitly
aware of this aspect of wording. Indeed, they could not be,
nor had they any need to be, aware of it. For them, thinking

[61] "Substanz und Akzidenz in der Eucharistielehre," *Zts. f. Kath. Theol.*
83 (1961), pp. 257–306. G. Ghysens, on the other hand, is also incorrect
in dissociating the way the fathers of the Council of Trent thought about
faith from their Aristotelian views, in which they expressed at least the
"remaining of the *species*" in a way as meaningful to themselves. See
"Présence réelle et transsubstantiation dans les définitions de l'Eglise
catholique," *Irén.* 32 (1959), pp. 420–35.

[62] *Concilii Tridentini Acta, op. cit.,* pt. 5, pp. 873–4, 876–7, 883–92,
906, 914, 916, 923, 926, 929, 950, 1010, 1013.

[63] Especially "remanentibus accidentibus sine subiecto" (*ibid.,* pt. 6, p.
131).

and experiencing as they did, it was not simply a question of "wording," but the only possible way of thinking meaning-fully as Catholics about the presence of Christ in the Eucha-rist, at least in connection with the "remaining of the species." That is why it is impossible for us to comprehend the content of faith of the declarations of the Council of Trent if we try to grasp the way in which the fathers thought about faith precisely insofar as they dissociated themselves from their "Aristotelianism." That would be an attempt to trace what Trent believed in isolation from its concrete faith—an attempt to catch *in flagrante delicto* a way of thinking about faith after having previously elimi-nated all the factors which might lead us to this capture. Only a generation of believers living at a later period in the development of human consciousness and therefore further removed from the Aristotelian metaphysical philosophy of nature in its medieval form—and capable at least of seeing this philosophy more clearly if they have not rejected it al-together—can be aware that this medieval mode of thought was historically conditioned and hence, in the concrete sense, a form of "wording" for what the Council of Trent was really trying to express. But, in that case, this later generation will not be able to grasp the genuine *content of faith* of the Council of Trent if they methodically set aside their own (and later) way of thinking. If we, living in the twentieth century, are to discover the geniune content of the Triden-tine faith in connection with Christ's presence in the Eucha-rist, we must also enter intimately into this content of faith, reassessing it and making it actual and present, because we can never really grasp it in its "pure state."

But we have not yet established apodeictically whether or not there is an important factor of "wording" in the Tridentine doctrine. We have seen that there were three "levels" in Thomas, for example, which were ultimately fused. Firstly, there was Thomas' affirmation of the unique presence of Christ that was "peculiar to this sacrament." Secondly, he affirmed a radical change or a change of the substance of bread and wine, which he personally (that is, when he was not engaged in translating his own most deeply held conviction into traditional terms) called a "change of being" (*conversio totius entis*). By this, he meant that the *reality* of bread was something quite different after the consecration—it became the body of Christ.[64] Thirdly, he made use of the Aristotelian theory of substance and accidents. Thomas distinguished these three levels in the concrete structure of his treatise and discussed them separately, passing from the first to the second and then on to the third. We can sum them up as the level of *faith* (the special eucharistic presence), the *ontological* level (the change of being or *trans-entatio*) and the level of *natural philosophy* (the *trans-substantiatio*). Ultimately, of course, these three levels

[64] "Conversio *totius entis*," "se extendens ad *totam naturam* entis"— "change of the *whole being*," "extending to the *whole nature* of the being" (*ST*, III, q. 75, a. 4). "Id quod *entitatis* est in una, potest Auctor entis convertere ad id quod est entitatis in altera"—"The Author of being can change what is *of the reality* in one into what is of the reality in the other" (*ST*, III, q. 75, a. 4, ad 3).

formed one single vision—as a believer, he thought about the dogma in ontological terms and in terms of natural philosophy. "Here I stand, I can do no otherwise!" He could not separate one from the other because if he did so the dogma of faith itself would be in danger for him. But then *we* are at once confronted with the question as to whether the ontological can and must not be preserved even if the level of natural philosophy is no longer serviceable for us. We are also faced with a second question—Does the level of faith also in fact imply the *ontological* level? Did not one theologian, Bishop Casellus, suggest in Trent itself (or rather, in Bologna) that it was right to speak of a "change," but that this should be thought of at the level of sacramentality or symbolic activity and thus be called a "sacramental change" (*conversio sacramentalis*)?[65]

It is *a priori* quite conceivable that anyone who has to reject the specifically Aristotelian character of the doctrine of substance and accidents (we are, after all, not bound by faith to an Aristotelian philosophy) may still be able to keep to an ontological "change," on the basis of which the answer to the question "What *is* that?" after the consecration can no longer simply be "It is bread." In such a case, it is perfectly clear that a demythologisation of this kind of the Aristotelian element in the Tridentine dogma is still completely faithful to the Catholic belief in the real presence of Christ in the Eucharist. But, in the light of the modern problem, we are obliged to ask the further question, leaving aside the consideration of the Aristotelian philosophy of

[65] See above, footnote 14 of this chapter.

nature (which, *as believers,* we might in any case just as well drop): Did Trent really mean to insist on an *ontological* aspect or does this too come within the scope of what at the present time may be called the aspect of *"wording"* of the Tridentine dogma? In my opinion, this question brings us to the very heart of the modern problem.

It is historically clear that theologians and the Church had already spoken of a "change of the substance" of bread and wine even before the Aristotelian doctrine of substance and accidents had penetrated into the West.[66] What is more, the Greek Fathers, Ambrose and the theologians of the Carlovingian period had, in their thinking, clearly followed a direction which led to the conviction that the Catholic view of the eucharistic presence could not be maintained without a *real* change of the bread (without any allusion to an Aristotelian philosophy of nature). The fathers of the Council of Trent were certainly informed about the way in which the Fathers of the Church conceived the eucharistic presence, at least in broad outline and without critical identification of individual authors. Centuries before the Latin Church had begun, in the late Middle Ages, to use the word *trans-substantiatio,* the Greek Fathers had been speaking of a *trans-elementatio* or *meta-stoicheiōsis* (the elements, *stoicheia,* of bread and wine, changing into Christ's body and blood). Why, then, should the Latin Church not speak of *trans-substantiatio?* a doctor of Paris, John Consilii, ex-

[66] See above, Denzinger 355, 416 and 430 (700, 784 and 802). See also above, the bibliography under footnote 1 of the introduction, and below under footnote 70 of this chapter.

claimed in a very sound argument.[67] Reference was made in the Council to Tertullian, Ambrose, Jerome, Cyprian, Gregory of Nyssa, Gregory Nazianzen, Basil, Augustine, Irenaeus and others.[68] The fathers of the Council were therefore able to conclude, "Although the word (transubstantiation) is of more recent date, the real faith (*fides et res*) is nonetheless very old."[69]

Of course, the fathers of the Council of Trent were not aware of the distinctive character of the patristic view of the eucharistic change. Although the Greek Fathers remained outside the Aristotelian influence in the first three centuries of Christianity especially, they had always spoken about a *radical change* of bread and wine; that is, into Christ's body and blood. In the ancient Western liturgies, the terms used in this context were *transformare, transfigurare, transfundere* and *transmutare*. The ancient Eastern liturgies used the terms *metapoieisthai, metaballesthai, metarrythmizesthai* and *metastoicheuousthai,* and these technical terms were derived from the Greek Fathers.[70] Let me give just one

[67] *Concilii Tridentini Acta, op. cit.,* pt. 5, p. 945. He referred to Theophylactus (*PG*, 123, 1307), but this brings us to as late as the eleventh century. In fact, the term can be found as early as in Gregory of Nyssa, *Oratio catechetica,* 37, 4, ed. Strawley, 151,8 – 152,8 (*PL,* 45, 97). Theophylactus was quoted again and again in Trent: *Concilii Tridentini Acta, op. cit.,* pt. 5, p. 884; pt. 5, pp. 874 and 915.

[68] *Ibid.,* pt. 5, pp. 874, 884, 915 and 944; pt. 7, p. 163.

[69] *Ibid.,* pt. 5, p. 945.

[70] As early as 1855, a study was written dealing with the terms used by the Greek Fathers for this change: E. Pusey, *The Doctrine of the Real Presence, as Contained in the Fathers from the Death of S. John the Evangelist to the Fourth General Council,* Oxford and London (1855), pp.

example, from Theodore of Mopsuestia: "Christ did not say, 'This is the *symbolum* of my blood,' but 'This is my blood,' a *change* of the wine takes place."[71] The ancient Church was as firmly convinced of a real change of the bread and the wine as was the medieval Church.

But the categories in which the ancient Church thought about this datum were rather different from those in which the Church thought about it later, because the former was more orientated in her thinking towards the ancient world.[72] The early Christian vision was much more dynamic—corporeal things were, for the earliest Fathers of the Church, what they were because they were controlled by Powers, and a change of a thing meant that other Powers seized it and took possession of it. They said therefore that a Christian was a person whose flesh had been seized by the Pneuma, by God.[73] Moreover, these Greek Fathers regarded material things as being "without qualities; they can invest them-

---

162–266. The same study was taken up again, more critically, by J. Betz, *Die Eucharistie in der Zeit der Griechischen Väter*, Pt. I-1, Freiburg i. Br. (1955), pp. 300–18.

[71] *Fragmenta in Matt.* 26, 26 (*PG*, 66, 713). See also Cyril of Jerusalem, *Catech. Mystag.*, 5, 7 (*PG*, 33, 1113 and 1116)—Cyril cited the miracle of Cana as a guarantee of this miraculous eucharistic *conversio, ibid.*, 4, 2 (*PG*, 33, 1097 and 1099); Gregory of Nyssa, *Oratio catechetica*, 37, 2, 3 and 4 (*PG*, 45, 93–7)—"by the power of the blessing, the nature of what we see is *transelementalised*"; Cyril of Alexandria, *Comm. in Matth.*, 26, 26 (*PG*, 72, 452–3); John Damascene, *De fide orthodoxa*, 4. 13 (*PG*, 94, 1144); John Chrysostom, *Homilia de proditione Judae*, 1, 6 (*PG*, 49, 380), *In Matth. homilia*, 82, 5 (*PG*, 58, 744).

[72] See J. Betz, *op. cit.*, p. 301.

[73] Irenaeus, *Adv. Haereses*, V, 9, 3, ed. Harvey, pt. 2, 343.

selves with all qualities as the Creator desires."[74] "To be changed" in the context of the Eucharist therefore meant that Christ, the Logos, took possession of the bread and the wine and made it his body and blood, that he appropriated them, making them his own body and blood. The terms *metaballein* and *metapoiein* used by the Greek Fathers for this eucharistic change meant precisely "to change by appropriating to oneself, by taking possession of." In this way, the Greek patristic view of the eucharistic change was in a sense an extension of the "hypostatic union," the incarnation. What was a problem of secondary importance for the scholastic theologians of a later period—that is, that the divinity of Christ, the Logos, was present "concomitantly" in the Eucharist—was the most important question for the Greek Fathers precisely because they regarded man's justification as a deification. The Logos took possession of the sacrificial gifts by the Holy Spirit's descent on them, just as he had taken possession of his body from the Blessed Virgin. The way the change took place was thus the same as that in which the Logos appropriated his body at the incarnation.

It was, so to speak, a cultic and sacramental incarnation of Christ—the Holy Spirit descended on the offering, "penetrated" the elements and made them the body and blood of Christ, and this could only take place within the mystery of liturgical worship. The Logos thus took possession of these sacrificial gifts of bread and wine, which then acquired a "pneumatic power" through being in the possession of

[74] Origen, *Contra Celsum*, 3, 41 (*GCS*, pt. 1, 237).

the life-giving Logos. The incarnation in this way continued
to be living and effective in a cultic and sacramental manner
in the Eucharist. In other words, the bread and wine were,
by virtue of the descent of the Holy Spirit, changed into the
"body-and-blood," in the body that was hypostatically of the
Logos. Instead of natural powers, the saving power of Christ
was now effective in the sacrificial gifts. In this way, the
bread and wine were, after the consecration, to be sacramental *forms* in which the body of the Logos *appeared*.
They had, in other words, lost their natural independence
as things of nature—they had been dispossessed of themselves (*de-substantiatio*) and possessed by the Logos, received
into the body of the Logos (*trans-substantiatio*).

The basic patristic intuition was the same as that of the
Tridentine dogma, but it was expressed within a different
framework of thought. The Greek Fathers did not in any
sense think of a substance situated "behind" the accidents.
In their view of the change of the substance of the bread
and wine, they did not see the substance as opposed to the
accidents, but in its independent being. The bread and wine
lost *this* substance and acquired a radically new independent
being or reality, that of the body of Christ, the saving organ
of the Logos. It cannot be denied that what we have here
is a real transubstantiation which was not conceived in
Aristotelian terms and which in a dynamic way possesses
great ontological density. Just as Trent sanctioned the word
transsubstantiatio in the sixteenth century, so did the Greek
Church also eventually sanction, in a seventeenth-century

synod, the word *metaousiōsis* (a non-patristic term, but a translation of the Latin *transsubstantiatio* and thus dependent on the Latin Church).

This all goes to make it quite clear that, although the fathers of the Council of Trent thought of the "change" (*conversio*) in Aristotelian terms, this Tridentine "change" does suggest a *reality* of which the early Church was also deeply convinced, but which she did not express in an Aristotelian context. This should be sufficient confirmation of the idea that canon 2 of the Council of Trent does suggest a reality *of our faith* which need not of itself be interpreted in the Aristotelian sense.

We must now take another datum into account. The *word* "transubstantiation" was without doubt partly formed with a biblical echo in mind. Medieval theology developed within the study of *Sacra Pagina* (Holy Scripture), the first branch to emerge being grammatical theology, the next dialectical and finally speculative theology. The terminology of theology was therefore interspersed with biblical words (from the Vulgate and other early Latin translations) even when the division between *lectura* (biblical exegesis) and *quaestio* (speculative theology) had gradually become established. Biblical words, about which a *quaestio* had previously been asked in the *lectura,* continued to be used in speculative discourses even if they no longer had any direct connection with the content of the original biblical text. The use of biblical words (often no longer directly associated with their biblical context) in independent speculation was a characteristic of medieval theologians who, in this sense—that is,

terminologically—thought "biblically." Now the Latin translation of the words "daily bread" in the Matthaean version
of the Our Father ("give us this day our daily bread," Matt.
6. 11) was *panis supersubstantialis*,[75] and it has struck me in
the Acts of the Council of Trent that theologians especially
made a connection between the idea of transubstantiation
and this "biblical" *panis supersubstantialis*. One of the
bishops, John Fonseca, in fact said explicitly that it was
heretical to deny transubstantiation, because it was contrary
to the Our Father, "da nobis panem supersubstantialem."[76]
Whenever early scholastic theologians who, especially since
the time of Boethius, had become familiar with speculations
about "substance" read these words in the Latin translations
of the Bible, their minds at once began to work like elec-
tronic brains, and they made connections. I have not made
a special study of this question, as there is still too much
material that is in manuscript and has not yet been published—it remains a "feeling" that is based on a few indica-
tions, which are nonetheless very suggestive. But I do feel
convinced that the Latin Bible in the early scholastic period
was partly responsible for the new word-formation "transubstantiation" and not the typically Aristotelian theory of
substance and accidents.[77]

[75] A rendering of the Greek *epi-ousion* which was translated in the
Latin version of Luke 11. 3 as *panis quotidianus*.

[76] *Concilii Tridentini Acta, op. cit.,* among other places, pt. 7, p. 150.
See also the statements of other bishops and theologians: pt. 7, pp. 129 and
140.

[77] The first time, as far as we know, that the word *transsubstantiatio*
was used was in the *Sententiae* of Roland Bandinelli, who later became

What, then, did "substance" mean in the tradition of the Church? Even in the patristic and the early medieval periods, this word had already had a long history that was independent of the precise relationship between substance and accidents. It was used in two ways. The prescientific meaning of the word was *reality,* as opposed to *appearance* or something abstract (an *ens rationis*). It was used to mean everything that suggested the idea of "firmness," "steadfastness" or "stability," just as we still refer to "something substantial" both in connection with, for example, a meal or a conference and in connection with the foundation of our faith, that the Epistle to the Hebrews called the *substantia* or *hypostasis* of "things hoped for," that is, the firm foundation (Heb. 11.1). In the Christian literature of the first centuries, substance therefore always indicated *reality.* In addition, the word substance also came to be used scientifically in connection with trinitarian and christological polemics. *Substantia* was here linked with the Greek word *ousia,* which originally also pointed to the "firmness of being" of the *reality.* An Aristotelian influence already made itself felt in the patristic period, with the result that a twofold (scientific) concept of substance became current in a theological context—the *substantia prima* or the concrete reality, the reality that is firm in its being, the existing reality, and the *substantia secunda* or an abstract formalisation of this

---

Pope Alexander III, thus between 1140 and 1153 (see ed. Gietl, p. 231). Bandinelli did not, however, put it forward as a neologism. It would seem that the word was formed in the school of Laon between 1100 and 1130. In the second half of the twelfth century it was in current use.

concrete reality (the so-called *essentia* or *quidditas ab-stracta*).

This twofold meaning caused a great deal of theological confusion (which we can ignore here). The result of these theological fluctuations was that the word "substance" was used in theology (especially in contrast to "person") both for a non-spiritual, concrete reality (*substantia prima* or *ousia prōtē*) and in the sense of "abstract essence."[78] Thus, someone (presumably Faustus of Riez) already referred in the fifth century to a change of visible things (bread and wine) into the substance of the body and blood of Christ.[79] In the theology of the Carlovingian and early scholastic periods, then, *substantia panis* simply meant the *reality* bread, not in itself in relation to the Aristotelian connection between substance and accidents. Quite apart from the Aristotelian philosophy of nature, the Church had for a long time been speaking about a *real* change or a change of the *substance* of the bread and wine in connection with the Eucharist. It is quite clear from the very first polemics about

[78] See, among others, J. de Ghellinck, "L'entrée d'essentia, substantia et autres mots apparentés dans le latin médiéval," *Arch. Lit. Med. Aevi* (Bull. du Cange) 16 (1942), pp. 77–112; *id.*, "Essentia et substantia. Note complémentaire," *ibid.* 17 (1942), pp. 29 ff. and 133 ff.; F. Erdin, *Das Wort Hypostasis,* Freiburg i. Br. (1939); F. Sassen, *De vraag naar het zijn in de eerste eeuwen der scholastiek* (Meded. Kon. Ned. Akad. van Wetensch.), Amsterdam (1937). See also H. de Lubac, *Corpus mysticum,* Paris (1944), pp. 171–6 and 243–8.

[79] See *PL,* 30, 272 (known to the theologians of the Middle Ages via the *Decretum Gratiani*). See also *PL,* 67, 1052–6 and *PL,* 100, 203. It was only from the time of the polemics against Berengarius in the eleventh century that *substantia* became a key-word in the doctrine of the Eucharist.

the eucharistic presence between Ratramnus[80] and Radbert[81]
in the ninth century (long before the polemics around
Berengarius in the eleventh century) that the sacramental
sign of the "bread"—in the sense in which the Church
understood the *signum* of this particular sacrament in contrast to the *signa* of the other sacraments—of necessity implied a *real* and, in this sense, substantial or radical change
of the bread. Even Ratramnus, branded as a heretic by Radbert, whose thought was rather strongly "sensualist," accepted a fundamental change of the bread, but emphasised
the sacramentally veiled character of this event (*in figura*).
Indeed, so much stress was laid on the "sign" that not only
was Christ's body and blood *referred to,* but this body and
blood was concretely and really present for me here and
now "in," "under," "via" or "through the medium of" (the
best formula was sought) the sacramental form of bread
and wine.

It was essential and fundamental to the dogma of faith
that there should be no *reality* bread after the consecration,
since, if the ultimate *reality* present in the Eucharist were
to be called bread, there would be simply bread (a reality
cannot at the same time be two realities!) and the eucharistic presence could only be conceived symbolically. The
whole of the Catholic life of faith was opposed to this. The

[80] See the critical edition by J. N. Bakhuizen van den Brink, *Rathram-
nus. De corpore et sanguine Domini,* Amsterdam (1954).

[81] Paschasius Radbertus, *De corpore et sanguine Domini* (PL, 120,
1267–1350); see J. Ernst, *Die Lehre des hl. Paschasius Radbertus von der
Eucharistie,* Freiburg i. Br. (1896).

fundamental reality that the Catholic faith affirms is, after all, "This here, this is my body," given to you as *spiritual* nourishment not only for your "soul" but also for your body. The affirmation of Trent in canon 2, that there is a fundamental, radical and, in this sense, substantial change of the bread, is a purely dogmatic datum of faith, confirmed by the whole tradition of the Church. It was only in an attempt to explain the "remaining of the species" that the theory of substance and accidents arose in the minds of the fathers of the Council, with the result that, speaking *traditionally* of the "substance" of bread, they inevitably produced a contrast between substance and accidents. Dogmatically, however, the "change of substance" as an affirmation of reality was contrasted exclusively with "only as in a sign or figure" and "only by efficacity" (canon 1). That was the immediate meaning of substance in the whole of the earlier dogmatic tradition.

Independent of the Aristotelian framework, then, the ultimate question is whether the Catholic view of the eucharistic presence can be thought of without a *real* and, in this sense, ontological change of bread and wine. Is this implication something that was necessary to thought in the Middle Ages, or is it clear from the affirmation of the whole of patristic thought which was orientated in the same direction and (despite "spiritualising tendencies" that were constantly arising) the whole of pre-Tridentine theology that it is primarily an inner ontological implication of the dogma of the eucharistic presence and *for this reason* a universally valid necessity—in other words, a dogmatic requisite of faith? The affirmation of the eucharistic presence is so closely bound up with the affirmation of a real change of bread and wine that the affirmation of this change is the concrete content of the dogmatic statement—the real Tridentine dogma as an affirmation of reality.

The Problem: What Is Reality?

We have, however, still not settled the hermeneutic problem. It is only now that we are faced with the central question, What is reality? In this problem, we should be careful to distinguish reality in a naively realist view of human knowledge from reality in an idealist theory of knowledge and to bear in mind that both these views are different from Merleau-Ponty's extension of idealism to include corporeality, from Sartre's or from De Petter's views of the *en-soi.* Let me give one example to make this clear.

The Calvinist theologian F. J. Leenhardt reacted against Zwingli's purely symbolic view of the presence of Christ in the Eucharist which had a considerable influence on later Reformed thought. Leenhardt wanted to retain the word transubstantiation, but to use it in the light of the Protestant view of reality. Reality, according to Leenhardt, is determined by the creative word of God ("the true reality of things is to be found in what God wants these things to be for the creature"[82]) and consists of a twofold relationship—

[82] F. J. Leenhardt, *Ceci est mon corps,* Neuchâtel and Paris (1955), p. 31.

its relationship to God and its relationship to the creature, man. The true reality of something is thus situated in what God gives to man through these things. The truth or reality of things is therefore not to be found *in* these things themselves, in what we, as men, see and experience of these things: "the substance of a reality is in the divine intention which is realised in it" (*ibid.*). Only faith, then, is able to grasp this substantial reality: "Only faith is capable of knowing what things are in God's will, what their destination is, their raison d'être, and that it is here that the essence of their being, their ultimate substance, is to be found" (*ibid*). If Christ himself said in the sovereign freedom of his power, "This is my body," this means that the "substance," the reality with which I am concerned in the Eucharist, is not bread for me—I who understand this reality as a believer— but the true body of the Lord with which I can nourish myself: "faith will acknowledge that this bread . . . no longer has the same substance."[83] From the human point of view, the bread remains inwardly unchanged—it is still ordinary bread. But for the eyes of faith, it is *really* no longer bread, but the body of Christ, given to me to eat. According to this ontology of faith, the bread is no longer ontologically bread, but the truly present body of the Lord. The "bread" is therefore more than simply the "sign of Christ's presence"— "the sign . . . *realises* this presence."[84] Christ, then, does not give us believers bread to eat, but really himself.

This view of reality is clearly very different from the

---

[83] *Ibid.*, p. 33.

[84] *Ibid.*, p. 36: "Le signe . . . réalise cette présence."

Catholic view. It is, of course, true that we would not dis-
agree with Leenhardt's primary affirmation, that God himself is the ultimate ground on which all reality is founded,
that reality is what it is by divine constitution. But the
Catholic view of reality cannot admit the "extrinsicism"
of the creative word of God. He claims in addition that
through this creative word things are what they are, in an
absolute and inward manner.[85]

But does Leenhardt's modern Calvinist view[86] of the real
presence imply a difference *in faith* from the Catholic religious view (and experience of the Eucharist) or merely a
difference *in ontology,* which is of no further interest to the
life of faith? I am of the opinion that, however different
philosophy and faith may be, our view of reality cannot
possibly be separated completely from our conviction of
faith. To make a division of this kind seems to me to be unjustified, because the judgement of faith is by definition a
judgement about reality, and a difference of opinion about
what constitutes reality naturally involves a difference in
faith—or at least it has an influence on the density of the

[85] Thomas' affirmation in this connection is still very meaningful:
"unumquodque dicitur bonum *divina bonitate*"—"each thing is said to be
good with the *divine goodness*" (that is Leenhardt's view), "nihilominus
unumquodque dicitur bonum similitudine divinae bonitatis *sibi inhaerente,*
quae est formaliter sua bonitas denominans ipsam"—"nonetheless each
thing is said to be good in the likeness of the divine goodness *inhering in
it,* which is formally its goodness by which it is thus named" (*ST,* I, q. 6,
a. 4).

[86] For a historical study of Calvin, see G. P. Hartveldt, *Verum Corpus.
Een studie over een centraal hoofdstuk uit de Avondmaalsleer van
Calvijn,* Delft (1960).

concrete sense of faith. Some accretions of the Catholic "devotion to the tabernacle" are certainly accretions, but they have nonetheless a specific orientation. They were able to develop in the first place only on the basis of the specifically Catholic view of reality, just as the specifically Zwinglian development of an evacuation from the Eucharist of the real presence of Christ had its origin in the Protestant view of reality. Basically, the Reformation wants to hold onto the reality of a specific presence of Christ in the Eucharist, but it is still hesitant about accepting the realism of Leenhardt or that of the Taizé community.[87] It is, then, possible to some extent to distinguish, in both the Catholic and the Protestant "accretions," the *orientation* of the fundamental views of both and therefore to sense the real danger to which each view is exposed through its basic tenets. In the meantime, both Catholics and Protestants are nowadays reacting against the accretions to their own basic tenets.

There is, then, a decided difference between the Catholic and the Protestant views of reality, and this difference has made itself felt in christology, in ecclesiology, in mariology, in the doctrines of grace and the sacraments and in eschatology, to mention only the most fundamental themes. A. Hulsbosch put his finger on an essential point when he said that Rudolf Bultmann saw reality one-sidedly as a *pure relationship,* that is, as a relationship which took on no form *in* the reality which is man and the creature.[88] For the Catholic, however, this relationship is *filled*—precisely in what the

[87] M. Thurian, *L'Eucharistie,* Neuchâtel and Paris (1959).

[88] "Het verstaan van de Schrift," *Ts. v. Theol.* 5 (1965), pp. 1–27.

creature is inwardly (I may even say, as a "secular" being), it is a transcendental relationship to God. Thus God's saving activity with regard to man is also primarily and totally a sovereign and free act of conferring grace, but this act is so real that "created grace" in man is, as it were, its other side. The creature does not need to give way to God when he approaches, as water has to give way to a piece of wood that is plunged into it. On the contrary, the creature is completely permeated by God without any withdrawal whatever. God is not a fellow creature who occupies his own space beside me and to whom I have to yield if he wants to occupy my space as well. He is, even when he confers grace, transcendent through interiority.

It is undeniably true that since the Counter-Reformation Catholic theologians have tended to fix their attention on this naturally *creative* aspect (gratuitously *ex nihilo* and therefore transcendant through interiority) that is present in all conferring of grace, and consequently they have often neglected to consider the most distinctive aspect of grace, the intersubjectivity between God and man (God's address to man and man's response in faith). In the case of the Eucharist too, the fundamental event—Christ's *de facto* giving of himself here and now, his real *presentation* of himself in the Eucharist—has all too frequently been lost sight of and the real *presence* as an "objective datum" has been given one-sided attention in isolation from this event. Once again, then, I should like to emphasise that this one-sided treatment is an accretion; nevertheless in itself it follows from what constitutes the basic, authentically Catholic meaning of the Eucharist—that is, the creative aspect that is present in every act in which God approaches man to confer grace on him. Have modern authors, who rightly emphasise that the Eucharist in Christ's hands is a symbolic act on the part of the man Jesus (the Son of God), given sufficient thought in this connection to the vital conviction of the Fathers of the Church (a conviction that has, unfortunately, lost much of its vitality for us) that the Eucharist was the work of the divine Holy Spirit, the *Spiritus Creator?*

The "ontological aspect" of the Eucharist, God's gift of salvation in Christ and thus his saving activity here and now in a sovereign free act of self-giving, is precisely this "creative aspect." This aspect may be regarded as "created grace," which is implicit in all God's communication of himself in grace, but which has an unexpectedly profound ontological density in this particular gift of himself in the Eucharist, since it takes hold of the secular reality of the bread creatively and is not simply a transcendent "naming from outside" which leaves the *secular* reality as it was before (those who accept this do not, after all, accept any transcendence *in* the interiority itself). And it is precisely *that* aspect which the Council of Trent indicated with the word *conversio* (the change of the bread), thus continuing the whole Christian tradition in a pure form. In the second canon, the Council made the datum of faith of this change, which was only implicit in the first canon, explicit. In other words, the presence of an *ontological aspect* in the *sacramental* giving of the bread is without doubt a datum of faith and not simply an aspect of "wording." The *reality* of Christ's gift of himself in the sacramental bread is involved here.

According to the Catholic view of revelation and thus of the whole order of salvation, grace itself comes to us in a historical, visible form, on the horizontal level of human history (and, included in this, on the level of the cosmos or the corporeal world) and not simply vertically, like rain falling from heaven. What comes to us from heaven—grace —in fact comes to us *from the world,* from human history with its secular environment. Our personal relationship with God in grace is at the same time a relationship of fellow-humanity and thus of orientation towards the secular world. In a cosmic piece of bread, grace is conferred on me by Christ in the Eucharist. But Christ's act of giving himself and of conferring grace precisely in and through the consecrated bread has a creative aspect, first and foremost not with regard to me, but *in* the gift of this bread as Christ's *sacramental* giving of himself—in its ultimate reality, this bread is therefore simply no longer bread—and then, through my communion in faith, also in me. The bodily activity of eating is therefore (for the believer, that is) a saving activity. The cosmic reality does not remain outside this process of grace, nor is it involved in it simply by an extrinsic word of God—the consecrated bread itself *is* the grace that is conferred here; that is, Christ himself in a sacrament to be eaten as a sacrificial meal, nourishment for the whole man. The secular world itself is intrinsically involved in Christ's gift of himself in the Eucharist and therefore—and this, in my opinion, brings us to the deepest meaning of the Tridentine dogma of transubstantiation (an analysis of the "meaning for me now" of this dogma will follow in a later chapter)—the secular world already *shares* in the eschatological situation of the glorified corporeality which will be deified entitatively. But we are still in the "already now" and "not yet" that characterises the period of salvation between the resurrection and the *parousia,* and the consecrated bread and wine therefore still belong, in their new meaning as "new creation" of the order of salvation, to "this old world" also. For this reason, transubstantiation contains two dimensions—a *change of being* of the bread and wine (in which Christ's glorified body is really offered through the Holy Spirit), but *within the terrestrial, but now* (through this change of being) *sacramental form* of bread and wine, which remain subject, in this secular world, to the terrestrial laws of corporeality (in this case, of the vegetable product of cultivation that we eat as bread and drink as wine in our daily lives). Transubstantiation thus has two dimensions of one and the same undivided reality. This is the essential meaning of the dogma.

In asserting, on the witness of the entire Christian tradition (in accordance with "Pneuma-christology"), that an ontological aspect is present in the Eucharist, a change of *being,* we should not forget that we are at the same time dealing here with an ontological aspect of a *sacramental symbolic activity* on the part of Christ and therefore with a profound objective reality of precisely this symbolic activity which is, of its nature, orientated towards the sacramental response of the believer. *A priori,* we ought not to look for realities in the Eucharist outside the sphere itself of sacramentality—to do so would be to leave the standpoint of faith and the Eucharist. This is, after all, our aim—the *sacramental parousia!* In this perspective, the "ontological dimension" or intrinsic reality of the consecrated bread, as Christ's sacramental giving of himself, may indeed be open to an interpretation which is different from that of scholasticism. Scholasticism had, after all, a tendency to look for the ontological aspect "in depth," so to speak *behind* the phenomena themselves, with the consequence that, in connection with anthropology, for example, the "substance of the soul" was given a greater ontological density than man's psychical activity as a person—as though a meaningful human action did not have a greater ontological depth than a *substantia animae* which had, as it were, sunk to the zero of its freedom and personal activity! It is impossible for a "substantialist" metaphysical view such as this, which had, in later scholasticism, assumed rather more daring proportions than in the earlier scholasticism of the High Middle Ages, to provide an intelligible interpretation of the unsuspected ontological depth in a human meaning given by the man Jesus, the Son of God, glorified in the Holy Spirit. But this is anticipating the following chapter.

The Eucharist is, of its very nature, an event of the period between the resurrection and the parousia, a period during which earthly realities become historical manifestations of the gift of grace here and now and—in the sacramental liturgy, within the mystery of the Church's community of grace led by its office; that is, especially in the Eucharist— are withdrawn from their secular independence, their "being themselves," to the extent of becoming the sacramental form in which the heavenly bodiliness of Christ himself— that is, of his real presence for me—appears. There is in the Eucharist, as distinct from the other sacraments, a specific earthly real presence of the Christ who is nonetheless heavenly and remains heavenly in the sacrament. It is, of course, a *sacramental* earthly presence, due to Christ's real act of making himself present *in* the gift of the holy bread placed at the disposal of all who wish to approach this sacrament in faith. For this reason, the true reality in the Eucharist is no longer bread, but simply the body and blood of Christ in a sacramental form—that is the content of the Tridentine dogma which will be examined theologically in the following chapter in the light of our modern attitude. This modern approach has already been embodied, implicitly and existentially perhaps, in the foregoing analysis of the Tridentine doctrine. Otherwise the dogma would simply have been re-presented mechanically, and the eucharistic presence would have been seen only within its medieval intellectual framework and not in its openness to a modern Catholic interpretation which at the same time remains faithful to the Catholic tradition. Apart from this modern approach we, as believers, should never be able to seize the full implications for us of our Catholic faith. After all, we simply cannot formulate our belief as Christians did in the Middle Ages, or even as the apostles did; yet it is the same faith which we possess and experience—exactly the same faith, but with the dynamic identity of a living faith which is caught up in the movement of history.

This dogma of transubstantiation as Christ's saving action of making himself present to us and of transforming from within the sacrificial gifts of earthly food (gifts which were already universally sacrificial symbols in the natural religions and raised by Israel to the level of symbols of the saving event of the Pasch), thus making of them a new creation, a saving sacrificial gift in time for eternity, must be so formulated now, in a modern theological way, that the new formulation does not contradict the original, inviolable datum of faith or minimise it.

II

A New Approach Towards the Formulation of Faith

LET ME REPEAT what I said when I was analysing the dogmatic significance of the Tridentine dogma of transubstantiation, namely, that an analysis of this kind should not be viewed in isolation. In this analysis, not only should we take into account the celebration of the Eucharist by the primitive Christian community and its reflection on it, as given to us in various stages in the Bible—we should also keep constantly in mind how the Church continued to celebrate and think about the Eucharist. Such an extensive programme cannot, however, be carried out within the framework of this book. I have therefore concentrated my attention on only one aspect of the Eucharist, which I regard as fundamental. The path we follow here may not be considered as the model of a theological approach. The hermeneutical question about the real nature both of the biblical way of speaking about the Eucharist and of the way in which the magisterium of the Church speaks about it must, of course, in any case be asked. Instead of making a full examination of the mystery of the Eucharist, however, we must confine ourselves to a specific analysis of Christ's presence.

What may become clear in this chapter is how the contemporary context of our life leads us to reinterpret the
world of ideas with which the dogma of transubstantiation
has come down to us, precisely in order to be able to preserve
in a pure form the basic meaning of the dogma and to make
it capable of being freshly experienced by modern man. It
is difficult to see how simply repeating the dogma word for
word in our present age could do anything but impose an
unnecessary and unjustified burden on our Christian faith.
If this were done, the concept of "mystery" would be
handled like a *deus ex machina,* and elements which in fact
belong to a way of understanding man and the world which
has been superseded and hence are, for us today, no longer
valid and no longer part of our experience would be presented as "mysteries."

The approach to transubstantiation by way of the philosophy of nature was still fairly sober in the scholasticism
of the High Middle Ages, but in post-Tridentine scholasticism the Christian faith was buried under man-made
mysteries and miracles, and this occurred above all in the
post-Tridentine treatise on the Eucharist. Here God was
held to make a number of different interventions. Firstly,
he had to make the substance behind the phenomenon
"bread" disappear; then he had to give a new and miraculous function to the "quantity" as the deputising bearer of
the material "qualities," which were thought to be objective.
To explain the real presence of the heavenly Christ, the
further miracle of "adduction," "production" or "reproduc-

tion" in the bread was necessary. This in turn required a new miracle, to explain how it was possible for Christ to remain in heaven and yet, at the same time, to dwell "in the host," even though this did not take place spatially. This speculation should ultimately have resulted in the problem (which was never in fact sorted out and was not really taken seriously, as the previous questions were) of whether a reverse transubstantiation did not have to take place when the eucharistic forms passed away, and Christ accordingly returned to heaven—which he had, however, never left!

We can smile about these learned speculations now and wonder whether they were of any use to the ordinary people of the Church. Perhaps what ordinary Christians did get from them was a sense of the reality of the conviction that Christ's presence in the Eucharist must not be emptied out and "spiritualised." Wariness of a "spiritual" interpretation of the eucharistic event was in any case deeply rooted in both the biblical datum and the Church's traditional experience of the Eucharist. These theologians did not work in vain. We should not forget that human intersubjectivity was at that time still not thematised, that man was still approached in the categories of natural philosophy, despite the counter-influence of Augustinian thought, and that ontology was still infected with cosmology. In such a time it was almost impossible to experience the pre-eminently *human* character proper to a religious meal. In a context of natural philosophy the *reality* of the Eucharist—stressed again and again throughout the whole tradition of faith against spirit-

ualising tendencies—was bound to acquire a specially physical colouration. Every attempt was made to establish the
value of the Eucharist as a reality, and this was fully justified
since the reality of the Eucharist was its saving value. But
the ontological dimension was sought *outside* the sacramentality of the Eucharist. However, natural philosophy having
been taken as a point of departure, the questions which
arose, with their interconnected arguments, resulted in a
structure of such complexity that the theologian slowly but
surely reached the conviction that the starting-point itself
was open to question. Finally, when a new age had brought
another way of thinking, his proper course seemed to reject
this starting-point entirely and set out from some other.

This, of course, is what always occurs where man's approach to reality is concerned—whenever the consequences
of a line of reasoning are seen to be unacceptable, the path
which has been followed is retraced to the point of departure
and a new beginning is made. If we do the same now in
our interpretation of Christ's presence in the Eucharist, we
must, however, be careful not to forget that, even though it
eventually found itself in a blind alley, the older theology
also set out with the basic intention of safeguarding the
reality of Christ's presence in the Eucharist.

We are therefore impelled to find a new point of departure for our approach to the eucharistic presence. In the
first place, I shall show, with reference to modern authors,
what this new point of departure is. The approach will not

be from the philosophy of nature, but from anthropology. It will therefore be a formally sacramental approach to the problem. If the new interpretations are situated within the context of the "history of ideas," it will be apparent that they form part of an organic growth and are evoked almost inevitably. This will provide us with an initial insight into these interpretations, will make us realise how necessary reinterpretation is and will make us sympathetic and open to these attempts, even though we shall not view them uncritically.

This of course raises the question as to whether the "metaphysical" interpretation which, worded in the language of natural philosophy, nonetheless forms an essential part of the Tridentine dogma of transubstantiation will consequently disappear. Or must we conclude to an antithesis between the metaphysical approach and the phenomenological?

Anyone who considers the constantly renewed theological interpretations, each with its period of coming into favour and its period of decline, may be inclined to be sceptical about any attempt to interpret how Christ is present in the Eucharist. Is not every speculation simply relative and, in comparison with the living Christian experience of the Eucharist, is not all thinking which aims to thematise the "how" of the eucharistic presence at the most secondary in importance? An attempt to answer this metaphysical scepticism will form the conclusion to this chapter.

Factors Heralding the New Approach

The Conflict between Aristotelianism and Modern Physics

It had already become clear in the period between the two world wars that transubstantiation was in need of reinterpretation. The facts of modern physics had shaken the neo-scholastic speculations about the concept of substance to their foundations. This heralded the change from an approach to the Eucharist by way of natural philosophy to the anthropological approach.

Even at the beginning of the century, the influence of modern physics had caused heated polemics in neo-scholastic circles about the Aristotelian concept of substance. The idea that there was a reality behind and outside the world of phenomena had lost much ground when Kant's criticism penetrated to scholasticism, which itself suffered hard blows deriving from Henri Bergson's difficulties against "substantialism." And when it was finally established, long before Merleau-Ponty, that what was perceived by the senses could not be regarded as an objective attribute of reality that was separate from our perception, the Aristotelian doctrine of substance and accidents had to be radically overhauled. The quantum theory in physics made many neo-scholastics realise that the concept *substance* could not be applied to material reality—or at the most that the whole of the cosmos could be seen as only one great substance. The concept substance gradually came to be reserved for personal beings.

But how, then, was the change of substance of bread and wine in the Eucharist to be interpreted?

The result of the positive natural sciences had unmistakable repercussions on the natural philosophy concept of substance[1] and thus on theology as well. An almost incalculable number of books and articles concerning the impact of the positive sciences on the traditional understanding of the Eucharist appeared between the two world wars.[2] A few theologians were inclined to construct a kind of "dogmatic physics," but more and more theologians came to realise that transubstantiation had no connection with these physical and chemical structures. The general view was that the change of the bread and wine was not physical but metaphysical, and the "physcial" approach was thus in principle superseded.

Initially, however, the ideas of natural philosophy continued to influence the ontological approach, although here too modern physics indirectly pointed to the new way. Because the theologians who were trying to link the findings of this new science to the concept of transubstantiation came to conclusions which offered no prospects and because their point of departure was that an ontological change could not

[1] See, among others, W. Büchel, "Quantenphysik und naturphilosophischer Substanzbegriff," *Schk.* 33 (1958), pp. 161–85.

[2] See, for example, J. Ternus, "'Dogmatische Physik' in der Lehre vom Altarsakrament," *St. d. Z.* 132 (1937), pp. 220–30; A. Maltha, "Cosmologica circa transsubstantiationem," *Angel.* 16 (1939), pp. 305–34; F. Unterkircher, *Zu einigen Problemen der Eucharistielehre,* Innsbruck (1938).

leave the physical reality intact, they themselves contributed most of all to the view that an understanding of the Eucharist in terms of natural philosophy was untenable. This gave rise to an entirely new tension between the metaphysical interpretation (divorced from the natural philosophy framework) and the sacramental interpretation, which in turn led to the real reinterpretation of the dogma.

The Rediscovery of the Sacramental Symbolic Activity

The Sacrament as a Sign. Theologians began to turn their thoughts in quite a different direction after the Second World War. The debate between the defenders of the "physical" and the ontological interpretations flared up again, especially in Italy, between 1949 and 1960,[3] but in fact a different question was already preoccupying most theolo-

[3] See especially the polemics between C. Colombo and F. Selvaggi: F. Selvaggi, "Il concetto di sostanza nel dogma eucaristico in relazione alla fisica moderna," *Greg.* 30 (1949), pp. 7–45; C. Colombo, "Teologia, filosofia e fisica nella dottrina della transustanziazione," *Scuola Catt.* 83 (1955), pp. 89–124; F. Selvaggi, "Realtà fisica e sostanza sensibile nella dottrina eucaristica," *Greg.* 37 (1956), pp. 16–33 and "Ancora intorno ai concetti di sostanza sensibile e realtà fisica," *Greg.* 38 (1957), pp. 503–14; C. Colombo, "Ancora sulla dottrina della transustanziazione e la fisica moderna," *Scuola Catt.* 84 (1956), pp. 263–88 and "Bilancio provvisorio di una discussione eucaristica," *Scuola Catt.* 88 (1960), pp. 23–55. See also C. Vollert, "The Eucharist: Controversy on Transubstantiation," *Theological Studies* 21 (1961), pp. 391–425 and J. T. Clark, "Physics, Philosophy, Transubstantiation, Theology," *Theological Studies* 12 (1951), pp. 24-51.

gians—that of the relationship between the metaphysical approach and the *sacramentality* of the Eucharist. The tendency to approach the Eucharist, not ontologically and via the philosophy of nature, but anthropologically became increasingly prevalent at this time. Viewed retrospectively, some of the neo-scholastic polemics about substance were often so bizarre that they quite inadvertently contributed a great deal to this change of approach.

Emphasis could again be given in post-war theology to the fact that the sacraments are first and foremost symbolic acts or activity as signs—"sacramentum est in genere signi"[4] —because a better understanding in the perspective of history had been reached with regard to the biblical and patristic concept of *sacramentum* and *mystērion* and of the scholastic elaboration of this concept. Reacting against the Reformation, the post-Tridentine theologians placed too much emphasis on the saving causality of the sacraments and on their function as "instruments" of grace. The value of the sacraments as signs—accepted by both Protestants and Catholics and therefore not a controversial issue—was in this way pushed into the background and, in the long run, the fact that the sacraments were not concerned with physical realities but with sacramental realities was almost forgotten. This was especially true of the Eucharist which,

[4] Thomas, *ST*, III, q. 60, a. 1–a. 3; see the commentary on this in *De sacramentele heilseconomie* I, Antwerp and Bilthoven (1952), in the light of the patristic *mysterium* (pp. 21–106) and the early scholastic *sacramentum-signum* (pp. 107–19) and the scholasticism of the High Middle Ages (pp. 119–25).

being just as much *in genere signi,* is not, after all, outside the sphere of sacramental symbolic activity. By affirming this now, nothing has in fact been said—or not said—about the special character of the eucharistic presence. But it is in any case a great step forward that this distinctive character is no longer sought outside or, so to speak, behind the sacramentality itself.

Even as early as 1946 it was possible to find a reappreciation of the "eucharistic sign" in an article by Y. de Montcheul throwing historical light on Bonaventure's doctrine of the Eucharist—more consistent in the working out of certain details of the character of the Eucharist as a sign than Thomas' treatment,[5] although Bonaventure like Thomas still thought within a framework of natural philosophy. The new sacramental interpretation was thus in sharp contrast with the "physical" approach, in which eucharistic realities were ultimately looked for outside the sphere of sacramentality. On close consideration, this means looking for a non-eucharistic reality with the intention of passing it off as an element of the sacramental. To this, I would say, with Thomas, "It is very harmful to speak out, in the name of faith, in favour of or against any theory which has nothing to do with faith."[6] Anyone who is opposed to the "physical"

[5] "La raison du permanence du Christ sous les espèces eucharistiques d'après Bonaventure et Thomas," *Mélanges théologiques* (series *Théologie,* no. 9), Paris (1946), pp. 71–82. In 1925, the revival of the sacramental idea was already anticipated by A. Vonier, *A key to the Doctrine of the Eucharist,* London (1925).

[6] "Multum autem nocet talia quae ad pietatis doctrinam non spectant, vel asserere vel negare quasi pertinentia ad sacram doctrinam" (*Resp. ad*

approach, then, is inevitably faced with the question, How can the character of the Eucharist as a sign be consistently upheld and the biblical datum which continues to live in the Church, that the Eucharist implies a very distinctive "real presence," at the same time be substantiated? To situate transubstantiation, the basis of this distinctive eucharistic presence, outside the sacramental level would be theologically unjustified. It must be situated in the sign itself, in *this* (eucharistic) sign, and the *realism* of transubstantiation, as recognised in the Tridentine dogma, must also be upheld. The metaphysical interpretation of transubstantiation must be dissociated from the categories of natural philosophy, while the fundamental realism contained in it must be apparent at the level of sacramental symbolic activity— as a *reality* appearing in a sign.

The New Anthropological Interpretation of the Religious Symbolic Act in General. Modern phenomenology has developed not an epistemology of the sign, but an anthropology of the symbolic act based on a view of man which is not dualistic. According to this anthropological conception, man is not, in the first instance, an enclosed interiority which later, in a second stage as it were, becomes incarnate in the world through bodiliness. The human body as such is indissolubly united with the human subjectivity. The human ego is essentially in, and related to, the things of the world. Man is only present to himself—a person—if he

Joa. Verc. de art. XLII, proem. *Opusc. Theol.,* ed. Marietti [1954] I, n. 771).

comes into relation with reality outside himself, and especially with other persons. Man can be in the world through
self-revelation in the body only by orientating himself towards his fellow-men. It is only by directing itself outwards
towards other persons and the world that the human interiority is able to become fully a person. It is in his body
that man reveals himself and becomes visible, perceptible
and public. In this sense we may say—with no dualistic implications—that the human body does not refer to a soul
situated *behind* it, it is not a *sign* of the spirit: it is, on the
contrary, this interiority itself made visible. Thus human
interiority is at the same time revealed and hidden. But this
does not mean that it is hidden *behind* the bodily modes of
expression. It is also revealed in a veiled manner, *in* the body.

Regarded this way, symbolic activity has come to be seen
in a very different light. A sign as such always refers to
something else which is absent. But man's bodiliness, with its
modes of expression, is the visible presence of the spirit,
however inadequate this disclosure may be (as dissimulation
shows). If what is referred to in a sign is really present, it
can never be so by virtue of the sign itself. The spirit, however, reveals *itself* in bodiliness. Therefore, the reality itself
can be experienced directly *in* human symbolic activity.
There is no need to infer *from* a sign that this points to a
different reality which may be signified, but is not really
present. Hence the phrase "symbolic meaning" is no longer
adequate to represent the powerful reality of human symbolic activity, which is a real presence of human interiority
in its forms of expression, patterns of behaviour and so on,

even though it never sufficiently coincides with these forms.

On the basis of these anthropological considerations, then, the sacraments can be dissociated from the material sphere of "things" and taken up into the personal sphere. They are interpersonal encounters between the believer and Christ.[7]

The Tridentine Concept of Substance

Because the renewed neo-scholastic study of transubstantiation came to nothing, an attempt has been made during the last ten years especially—under the influence of the rediscovery of the real sphere in which the sacraments operate— to approach the eucharistic presence in an entirely new, phenomenological way. (This will be more fully discussed later.) As a result, several theologians have attempted to answer, in the light of a new "understanding of the world," the question as to precisely what the Council of Trent meant by "the substance of bread."[8] E. Gutwenger[9] regarded it as a foregone conclusion that the Tridentine fathers, in view of their appeal to the Council of Constance, wanted to express the dogma in Aristotelian concepts and thus that they to some extent consecrated these as *praeambulum fidei*.

[7] See, among others, my book *Christ the Sacrament of the Encounter with God* (London and New York, Sheed and Ward, 1963).

[8] This has been discussed in detail in the first chapter. I have only introduced the subject again here as a factor which led to this new approach.

[9] "Substanz und Akzidenz in der Eucharistielehre," *Zts. f. Kath. Theol.* 83 (1961), pp. 257–306.

G. Ghysens,[10] on the other hand, maintained that the Tridentine fathers completely dissociated themselves from the Aristotelian concept of substance, whereas Karl Rahner[11] claimed that no ontological interpretation of the eucharistic presence was contained in the definition of the dogma, but that the aim of the dogma was to state in *terms of logic* the same thing the Bible said, although in different words. As a result of my renewed study of the acts of the Council of Trent, I came to the conclusion, expressed in the first chapter of this book, that the mutually contradictory theses of Gutwenger and Ghysens were not based on a true hermeneutics of the Church's magisterial utterance. The dogma was thought out and expressed in "Aristotelian" categories, but the strictly Aristotelian content of these categories was not included in what the dogma intended to say. Christ's real presence in the Eucharist is therefore not tied to Aristotelian categories of thought.

Because, on the one hand, these concepts were becoming quite remote from modern existential thought and because, on the other hand, many theologians still continued to connect the dogma intimately with the Aristotelian philosophy of nature,[12] an uneasiness came to be felt about the concept

---

[10] "Présence réelle eucharistique et transsubstantiation dans les définitions de l'Eglise Catholique," *Irén.* 32 (1959), pp. 420–35.

[11] "Die Gegenwart Christi im Sakrament des Herrenmahls," *Schriften zur Theologie,* pt. 4, Einsiedeln (1960 ff), pp. 357–85.

[12] It is clear from G. J. Morsch's book, *De transsubstantiatie. Wijsgerig-theologische verhandeling,* Schiebroek (1938), that this view was still very characteristic of the pre-war Catholic idea of transubstantiation in the Netherlands. All the same, this work, in common with those by most

of transubstantiation. This uneasiness was made more acute by increasing ecumenical contacts with Protestant thought. In order to safeguard the dogma itself, it was necessary to reinterpret the dogmatic datum.

The Manifold Realisation of the One "Real Presence" of Christ

A fourth factor which gave rise to a reinterpretation of the dogma was the renewed insight into the fact that Christ's "real presence" should not be restricted to his presence in the Eucharist. This identification of Christ's real presence with his presence in the Eucharist goes back only to the time of Duns Scotus. The practice of returning to biblical and liturgical sources led to the official recognition, in the Constitution on the Liturgy (c. 1, n. 7) and the encyclical *Mysterium Fidei,* of the manifold intensity of the one real presence of Christ. Christ—and indeed, not only his activity or his power, but the person of Christ himself, since a presence is always personal—is really present in the service of the Word and in the liturgical assembly of the faithful. He is also really present in anyone who is in a state of grace. He is really present in the sacraments, and finally he is also really present in the Eucharist. In each of these cases, there is a *distinctive density* of Christ's real presence. In each case,

---

genuine Thomists of that time, was a welcome reaction against the doctrine of "adduction," "production" and "reproduction" of the later, post-medieval scholastics.

the proper character of this presence must be separately determined.

In the new approach to the distinctively eucharistic presence of Christ, an attempt is made above all to situate this presence within the sphere of Christ's real presence in the believer and in the whole believing community. In this way, the early Christian view can be recovered in its full dimensions—the distinctively eucharistic presence is directed towards bringing about Christ's more intimate presence in each individual believer and in the community of believers as a whole. The eucharistic presence is thus no longer isolated. We no longer say, "Christ is there," without asking for whom he is present. This distinction between a matter-of-fact "being there" and a presence in the sense of personal, and therefore interpersonal or reciprocal, presence has been suggestively formulated by P. Schoonenberg.[13] This reorientation also brings us closer to the real meaning of the dogma of Trent, which said that the Eucharist was instituted to be consumed,[14] in other words, that through the sacred medium of the sacramental meal Christ would dwell more intimately in our hearts, and the living community of believers, gathered around Christ as the bond, would be brought closer together.

[13] "De tegenwoordigheid van Christus," *Verbum* 26 (1959), pp. 148–57; "Een terugblik: ruimtelijke, persoonlijke en eucharistische tegenwoordigheid," *ibid.*, pp. 314–27; and a later article, "Christus' tegenwoordigheid voor ons," *Verbum* 31 (1964), pp. 393–415. See also R. Mehl, "Structure philosophique de la notion de présence," *Rev. Hist. Phil. Rel.* 38 (1958), pp. 171–6.

[14] "Ut sumatur institutum": *Denzinger* 878 (1643). See also 938 (1740).

The Desire for Christian Unity

Since World War II the idea that non-Catholic communities might be recognized as Churches has been gaining ground among Catholics, and the view was confirmed by the Second Vatican Council. This has served to point up in a particularly painful way the abnormality of the situation in which Christianity has been placed by the divisions in the one Church of Christ. But at the same time it has contained for Catholic theologians the implication that Christian experience outside the Catholic Church is also a *locus theologicus,* a place which provides material for theology. The Protestant experience of the Eucharist must therefore be taken into consideration by Catholic theologians. It is only in dialogue with Protestants that a truly Catholic interpretation of this datum of faith is completely meaningful. All Christians have to learn from each other—it is no longer possible for one Christian community to exclude another *a priori.*

It is a striking fact that Protestant theologians have also been looking for a new interpretation of the Eucharist since the Second World War, as a reorientation of their own tradition. Calvin and Luther especially had advocated a clear realism in connection with the celebration of the Eucharist, but the Protestant tradition was strongly influenced later on by the rather spiritualistic view of Zwingli.[15] Leenhardt and

[15] See, among others, F. J. Leenhardt, *Le sacrement de la Sainte Cène,* Neuchâtel (1948) and especially *Ceci est mon corps* (Cahiers théologiques, no. 37), Neuchâtel and Paris (1955); M. Thurian, *L'Eucharistie,* Neuchâtel and Paris (1959); G. Deluz, J. P. Ramgeyer and E. Gaugler, *La Sainte-*

Thurian especially have reacted against this view. Both these theologians are convinced Protestants, but they are very open to ecumenism, and they have given a non-Aristotelian interpretation of what they have nonetheless called a real transubstantiation.[16] Catholic exegetes were able to go a long way with their interpretations, although they were critical of certain essential points.[17] In this way, ecumenical dialogue about the Eucharist has become much more real, not only because Protestants have been moving in a "Catholic" direction (otherwise the dialogue would have been one-sided), but also because Catholic theologians have become more understanding and sympathetic towards this Protestant approach, which, since it was not coloured by the Aristotelian philosophy of nature, was in harmony with the post-war developments in Catholic theology. These Protestant stimuli (and protests) have certainly been instrumental in helping the Catholic theology of the Eucharist to emerge from the impasse into which the traditional approach based on natural philosophy had led it between the wars.

Cène, Neuchâtel and Paris (1945); C. W. Mönnich and G. C. van Niftrik, *Hervormd-Luthers Gesprek over het Avondmaal,* Nijkerk (1958); W. L. Boelens, *Die Arnoldshainer Abendmahlsthesen,* Assen (1964). See also J. F. Lescrauwaet, "Een nieuwe reformatorische studie over de Eucharistie," *Jaarboek 1960 Werkgen. Kath. Theol. Nederl.,* Hilversum (1961), pp. 109–24; S. G. Trooster, "De eucharistische werkelijke tegenwoordigheid van Christus in de hedendaagse protestantse en katholieke theologie," *Jaarboek 1962 Werkgen. Kath. Theol. Nederl.,* Hilversum (1963), pp. 113–36.

[16] See my concise analysis of Leenhardt's work especially in the first chapter of this book, pp. 76f.

[17] See especially P. Benoit, *Rev. Bibl.* 63 (1956), pp. 575–83.

If I have not mentioned all the factors which have stimulated the new approach to the Eucharist in Catholic theology, I have at least noted the five most important.

The New Point of Departure for the
Interpretation of the Eucharistic Presence

Catholic theology did not proceed at once to follow an anthropological course in approaching the question of the Eucharist when it had forsaken the Aristotelian philosophy of nature. There was a transitional period, in which what we may call simply the "metaphysical" interpretation, without any content of natural philosophy, prevailed. This movement sought the solution to the problem in the distinction between the *noumenon* and the *phenomenon*—that is, between the reality itself and the form in which it appears.[18] In this way, once more the very essence of the older Thomistic view was touched upon. The unity between the metaphysical and the sacramental aspects was, however, still insufficiently clear here, and the relationship between the phenomenal and the so-called "noumenal" aspects was not

[18] L. Godefroy, "Eucharistie," *Dict. Théol. Cath.,* pt. 5 (1939), col. 1349; J. H. Walgrave, "Transsubstantiatie," *Theol. Wdb.,* pt. 3, Roermond and Maaseik (1958), col. 4593–9; H. Verbeek, "De sacramentele structuur van de eucharistie," *Bijdr.* 20 (1959), pp. 345–55; S. Trooster, "De eucharistische werkelijke tegenwoordigheid van Christus," *ibid.;* A. R. van de Walle, "De hedendaagse reflectie op de eucharistische tegenwoordigheid in haar pastoraal-liturgische consequenties," *Ts. v. Lit.* 48 (1964), pp. 200–9.

closely analysed. The direction in which these theologians were moving did, however, seem to offer good prospects.

When I was studying in France in 1945 and 1946, transubstantiation was a subject of animated discussion among the students. The professor of dogmatic theology, a man well on in years but nevertheless very openminded, observing that the students could no longer find a place for his Thomistic doctrine of transubstantiation (which was itself a reaction against the post-Tridentine theology), allowed them to air their own views in seminars. Even then, words like "transfunctionalisation" and even "transfinalisation" could be heard in these discussions—the idea being that it was not the physical reality of the bread, but its function and meaning that were substantially changed. These discussions were not yet connected with modern phenomenology, which had, at that time, hardly begun to influence Catholic thought, but were prompted by the difficulties experienced in connection with the Aristotelian concept of substance as a result of modern physics and Bergson's criticisms.

The first theologian to rise above both the physical and the purely ontological interpretations and to situate the reality of the eucharistic presence in the sacramental presence was, without any doubt, J. de Baciocchi.[19] He accepted an ontological depth in transubstantiation, but placed this on the sacramental level. He did in fact use the terms trans-

[19] "Présence eucharistique et transsubstantiation," *Irén.* 32 (1959), pp. 139–61; written before this: "Les sacrements, actes libres du Seigneur," *Nouv. Rev. Théol.* 83 (1951), pp. 681–706; "Le mystère eucharistique dans les perspectives de la Bible," *Nouv. Rev. Théol.* 87 (1955), pp. 561–80; see also his recent book *L'Eucharistie,* Paris (1964).

functionalisation, transfinalisation and transsignification.[20] The ultimate reality of things is not what they are for our senses or for the scientific analysis that is based on this, but what they are for Christ. Christ's power as Lord makes all things be for him. If, therefore, Christ really gives *himself* in bread and wine, God's good gifts, then an objective and fundamental change has taken place, a transubstantiation— bread and wine become *signs* of Christ's real gift of himself.[21] De Baciocchi was reacting here against the concept of a substance situated *behind* the phenomenal world. "The gift of bread and wine is changed by Christ into the gift of his body and blood," and this changes the reality of the bread.[22] This was the first attempt by a Catholic theologian[23] to synthesise "realism" (transubstantiation) and "the sacramental symbolism in its full depth of meaning."[24]

It would seem that, with these views, the interpretation based on the Aristotelian philosophy of nature was com-

[20] "Christ's word, without altering these gifts as far as their empirical purport is concerned, entirely changes their *social and religious destination*" (article of 1959, *Irén.* 32, p. 150); "because the *new function* is *really* exercised, Christ making himself present and truly giving himself, the change of bread cannot be reduced to a subjective fact in the believer" (*ibid.*).

[21] "What is at issue here is not so much a metaphysical or, above all, a physical characteristic as Christ's absolute and creative sovereignty over all things" (article of 1955, *Nouv. Rev. Théol.* 83, p. 577).

[22] *Ibid.*, p. 577.

[23] Thomas Sartory had, however, already expressed several of these ideas, which were later included in his book, *Die Eucharistie Im Verständnis der Konfessionen,* Recklinghausen (1961).

[24] De Baciocchi, article of 1955, *Nouv. Rev. Théol.* 83, p. 578.

pletely superseded and the anthropological approach was already recognisable. It is, however, remarkable that this reinterpretation was not worked out until after 1950. This was the year in which the encyclical *Humani Generis* appeared, which denounced the opinion of certain theologians who maintained that transubstantiation was based on an outdated philosophical concept of substance and therefore had to be corrected in such a way that the real presence of Christ was reduced to a kind of symbolism, in which the consecrated hosts were simply efficacious signs of the *spiritual* presence of Christ and of his intimate union with his mystical body and its members. But I have never been able to discover a purely symbolical interpretation of the Eucharist in Catholic theology prior to 1950. Rome's criticism is probably based on a misunderstanding. Together with other theologians of the *Nouvelle Théologie* who favoured the practice of going back to original sources, Henri de Lubac had shown that both the early scholastic theologians and those of the High Middle Ages stressed not Christ's eucharistic presence (*res et sacramentum*), but the unity of all believers on the basis of a eucharistic communion with Christ (*res sacramenti*), the mystical body.[25] Thomas Aquinas also explicitly postulated that the saving power of this sacrament is ultimately situated in the real presence of Christ in the believing community itself.[26] The rediscovery of this datum

[25] *Catholicisme. Les aspects sociaux du dogme* (Unam Sanctam, no. 3), Paris (1938), pp. 56–74. See also *Corpus mysticum* (Théologie, no. 3), Paris (1944), 1949, especially pp. 295–339.

[26] *ST*, III, q. 73, a. 1, a. 3 and a. 6. For the difference between *res et*

has in fact supported the new interpretations. Whatever the
case may be, De Baciocchi was radically opposed to any
purely symbolic interpretation. Post-war Catholic theologians, who had rediscovered the sacrament as a sign, have
never again left the path that was first followed by De
Baciocchi, the path of synthesis between realism and sacramentality—two poles between which theologians have been
trying to find an equilibrium since the ninth century.

In Belgium, A. Vanneste, clearly inspired by De Baciocchi
and by Leenhardt's *Ceci est mon corps,* tried to make transubstantiation intelligible, but without appealing either to
philosophy or to cosmology or even to phenomenology.[27]
His point of departure was the creation, the fact that the
ultimate meaning of things comes from God. He made a
distinction, not between substance and accidents or between
the *noumenon* and the *phenomenon,* but between what
things are for God (and for the believer) and what they
are for our secular experience as men. Man does not give
things their ultimate meaning. If God gives a different destination to this bread, then it *is* metaphysically something
different: "philosophically too, the bread is no longer bread."

---

sacramentum and *res sacramenti*, see *ST,* III, q. 73, a. 2, a. 3 and a. 4;
q. 82, a. 2, ad 3; q. 83, a. 4.
[27] "Bedenkingen bij de scholastieke transsubstantiatieleer," *Collat. Brug.
Gand.* 2 (1956), pp. 322–35; Vanneste's review of Leenhardt's book, published in 1955, also appeared in the same journal, *Collat. Brug. Gand.* 3
(1957), pp. 270–3; "Nog steeds bedenkingen bij de transsubstantiatieleer,"
ibid. 6 (1960), pp. 321–48, written in reply to O. Schelfhout's attack,
"Bedenkingen bij een nieuwe transsubstantiatieleer," *ibid.* 6 (1960),
pp. 289–320.

In Germany, a new approach to transubstantiation was more fully explored in a symposium on the Eucharist held at Passau on the seventh to tenth of October, 1959. In the published account of the lectures and discussions,[28] the papers read by L. Scheffczyk[29] and B. Welte[30] are especially representative. Scheffczyk took as his point of departure the biblical belief in creation, which related the material reality as well as the spiritual to salvation, maintaining that at the deepest level the *being* of things was, in the Bible, a sign and symbol of spiritual and divine realities. This is worked out especially in connection with man and applied in all its depth to the man Jesus, the Son of God, so that the material substance in the Eucharist is fully sign. Although he did not use the word, Scheffczyk, like De Baciocchi, stated that a real transubstantiation must be a transsignification, which is a transfinalisation. B. Welte offered a more fully worked out analysis. His starting-point was that personal and spiritual relationships are more real than physical and material relationships. He therefore viewed bread and wine in the Eucharist in the light of their relationships. Being, being true and being good ("having meaning for") are, in the authentically Thomistic view, interchangeable. In their own *being,* things have a meaning for someone (God, man), an original meaning which belongs to the reality itself, since,

[28] *Aktuelle Fragen zur Eucharistie,* ed. by M. Schmaus, Munich (1960).

[29] "Die materielle Welt im Lichte der Eucharistie," in Schmaus, *op. cit.,* pp. 156–79.

[30] "Zum Vortrag von A. Winklhofer. Zum Referat von L. Scheffczyk," in *ibid.,* pp. 184–94. Reprinted as "Zum Verständnis der Eucharistie" in B. Welte, *Auf der Spur des Ewigen,* Freiburg i.Br. (1965), pp. 459–67.

without this "having meaning for," something is not what it
is. This transcendental "having meaning for" is made particular in concrete forms. A chemical substance may be
nourishment, but it may also be fuel. If this relationship is
changed, the being itself of a thing changes. A Greek temple
is something different for its builders, for those who worship
in it and for modern tourists. Man himself is essentially involved in this change of relationship, but it is not completely
dependent on him—the *being* itself of things changes when
the relationship is altered. It is therefore possible to say that
the temple has undergone a "historical transubstantiation."
There are also relationships which are *brought about* by
man. In such cases, *what* the being concerned really *is* is
authoritatively determined. A coloured cloth is purely deco-
rative, but if a government decides to raise it to the level of
a national flag, then the same cloth is really and objectively
no longer the same. Physically, nothing has been changed,
but its being is essentially changed. Indeed, a new meaning
of this kind is more real and more profound than a physical
or chemical change. In the case of the Eucharist too, a new
meaning is given to the bread and wine, not by any man,
but by the Son of God. The relationship which is brought
about by the Son of God is, because it is divine, binding in
the absolute sense and determines the being of the Eucharist
for the believer. Anyone who does not believe, and consequently does not see it in this way, places himself outside
the reality which is *objectively* present—he is outside the
order of being.

Welte put forward this idea as a working hypothesis. He

was in any case the first to elaborate in some detail a modern interpretation of transubstantiation—a change of the being itself (*conversio entis*) that is much more objective than physical changes, but on the level of giving meaning.

In the Netherlands in 1960, J. Möller, without looking for an ontological basis, put forward an existential and phenomenological interpretation[31] in which the reality of Christ's "giving of himself in the gift" was for the first time painstakingly analyzed phenomenologically. Although these analyses were not closely enough related to the specifically eucharistic context, they are nonetheless worthy of careful consideration by theologians.

The years 1964 and 1965 marked the beginning of a new phase in the reinterpretation of Christ's real presence in the Eucharist. By this, I mean above all that it was then that the new ideas which had been developed in different countries, especially during the ten years following the publication of *Humani Generis* in 1950, became widely known in the Church as a whole. Various theologians presented their views to the Catholic world, in England and the Netherlands especially, in a less academic way and with new shades of meaning.

In England, Charles Davis cautiously suggested a new anthropological interpretation that was in harmony with that of De Baciocchi.[32] In accordance with the general tend-

---

[31] "De transsubstantiatie," *Ned. Kath. St.* 56 (1960), pp. 2–14; "Existentiaal en categoriaal denken," *ibid.*, pp. 166–171, in reply to J. Kors' criticism, "De transsubstantiatie," *ibid.*, pp. 153–65.

[32] His latest publication is the one most easily accessible: "Understand-

ency away from the categories of natural philosophy and towards anthropological thinking, he based his argument concerning both grace and the sacramental life not on objective categories, but on interpersonal categories. Davis attempted to define more precisely the distinctive character of the eucharistic presence, which had, in his opinion, also to be interpreted in personal terms—that is, within the category of the interpersonal encounter between Christ and the believer—and to determine in this light what, so to speak, the "real presence" is *in itself* (directed, of course, towards this personal encounter) in the eucharistic bread and wine. It is the first stage of what must become a *reciprocal* presence and of what de facto also makes this reciprocal presence possible. Expressed in scholastic terms, it is the *res et sacramentum,* the first stage of the real presence, of which the *res tantum* is the completion. There is therefore an identification with the *object* and not with an action, although this is certainly assumed.[33] It is a substantial identity and therefore a "substantial presence." "Substantial" here means the manner of being present which has its origin in the identity with an object. This object, the eucharistic bread, is Christ. "As symbolic it embodies the reality it manifests." The reality itself of an object undergoes a change and, for this reason, there is no "consubstantiation," but a real transubstantiation. The identity is, however, not complete. Noth-

---

ing the Real Presence," *The Word in History: The St. Xavier Symposium,* ed. T. Patrick Burke (New York, Sheed and Ward, 1966), pp. 154–78.

[33] In his first articles in *Verbum* (1959), P. Schoonenberg also stressed this aspect.

ing is changed visibly and empirically, and what we perceive is not a deception. If the reality were changed empirically, there could be no question of sacramentality.

Davis does not, however, explain this by using the Aristotelian twin concept of substance and accidents. The change cannot, in his opinion, be situated at a non-empirical, physical level, separate from the personal and sacramental encounter with Christ, and he therefore proposes that the change concerns the reality the bread has as a "human object." There are objects which only have reality and meaning *for man* and are as such made by him for his needs, plans, self-expression and communication with others. These remain "external" realities (in this sense, an "ontological" reality as bread), but they are no longer "things of nature." Thus, the unity that we call bread is unintelligible without its relationship to man—it is only an agglomeration of diverse constituent parts. To this agglomeration transubstantiation gives a new *human unity,* a new meaning or relationship to man. The real, ontological meaning of the bread, that is, the bread itself, is thus radically changed—it is no longer orientated towards man as bread. A new pattern of unity is brought about, a new relationship to man, even though nothing is changed physically and the elements nourish the body as all bread does. A new object comes into being—the sacrament in which the reality of Christ is the *formally* constitutive element ("the substance as it were") together with the other elements which, subordinated to this new reality of Christ, are the *sign* of this reality and the *medium* by which it becomes accessible to us. The "new object" is thus the sacrament of Christ's body and blood.

Davis insists that the datum of Christ's presence in the Eucharist does not mean that he is, as far as we are concerned, absent outside the Eucharist. He is close to us in an even more intimate manner in the life of grace than he is in the tabernacle. Christ's real presence in the Eucharist therefore only finds its completion in the reciprocal encounter that takes place between Christ and ourselves. Davis' view thus amounts to an *ontological* "transfinalisation" and "transsignification," even though he does not in fact use these words. The basic meaning of the dogma of transubstantiation is guaranteed by Davis, but without the Aristotelian wording.[34]

In the Netherlands, the theologians P. Schoonenberg[35] and L. Smits[36] have moved in rather a different direction,

[34] It would be interesting to study the non-Aristotelian interpretations of transubstantiation (in the sense of a kind of "transsignification") among Anglo-Catholic authors writing since 1900. Some Anglo-Catholic views—especially those of Charles Gore, who wrote a book on the Eucharist in 1901—are set out in the completely revised edition of E. L. Mascall's *Corpus Christi,* London (1965[2]), especially on pp. 227-45.

[35] P. Schoonenberg, articles in *Verbum* (see above, footnote 13 of this Chapter); see also "Eucharistische tegenwoordigheid," *De Heraut* 95 (1964), pp. 333-6; "Nogmaals: Eucharistische tegenwoordigheid," *ibid.* 96 (1965), pp. 48-50; articles in *De Tijd* (21 December, 1964) and *De Volkskrant* (Maundy Thursday 1965).

[36] L. Smits, "Nieuw zicht op de werkelijke tegenwoordigheid van Christus in de Eucharistie," *De Bazuin* 48 (1964-5), no. 9 (28 Novem-

which they prefer to characterise, as equivalent to transubstantiation, as "transsignification" or "transfinalisation." Schoonenberg stresses above all that personal presence, in contrast to spatial presence, is identical with personal communication and is brought about by this. It is a self-communication of a person and a corresponding reception of this communication—in other words, a reciprocal self-communication in which the one person is himself for the other. This is reflected even in spatial presence—it always implies *activity,* the influence of one on the other. Personal presence is corporeally "mediated." It is visibly realised in signs. It is free self-disclosure and spiritual openness in bodiliness. Thus "the material activities of human bodies or things acquire a new dimension—they become *signs* of persons. . . . All making known or perception becomes a sign of revelation and faith, an active sign of human community, the manifestation and cause of personal presence."[37]

This interpretation properly stresses the fact that there are different degrees of personal presence. The two basic forms of personal presence are the presence that is *only offered* and the presence that is *also received* as a gift. "The only complete personal presence is that which is both given and accepted. That which is only offered, but is not (yet)

ber, 1964), pp. 3–4; "Beantwoording van vragen en opmerkingen aan p. Smits," *ibid.* 48 (1964–5), no. 23 (13 March, 1965), pp. 4–6; "Van oude naar nieuwe transsubstantiatieleer," *De Heraut* 95 (1964), pp. 340–5; *Vragen rond de eucharistie,* Roermond and Maaseik (1965).

[37] Article in *Verbum* 31 (1964), p. 405; see above, footnote 13 of this chapter.

accepted is a secondary presence, which is orientated towards
the first as its aim and completion."[38] There is also personal
presence which does not come about directly by "mediation" of the human body,[39] but by mediation of even more
alien material things, such as a letter, a souvenir or a gift.
In this context, however, these things become *signs*. "They
have a new and deeper being, being as signs, which communicates the personal presence. It is almost possible to say
that they are transubstantiated."[40]

Schoonenberg's analysis, of which I have given only a summary of a few main points, may be regarded as generally
acceptable to modern existential thought. It is quite possible
to say that the contemporary image of man and the world
is taken as much for granted in modern theology as the
Aristotelian image of man and the world was, broadly
speaking, in the theology of the second half of the thirteenth
century. This new understanding of man and the world
forms, in a less thematised way, the background to all attempts to reinterpret the Tridentine dogma, including, for
example, those of Charles Davis and Luchesius Smits.

After having applied this datum to the man Jesus, as
God's personal presence among us, Schoonenberg goes on

[38] *Ibid.*, pp. 406-7.

[39] This cannot properly be called a mediation, because this "medium"
of personal presence is not situated *behind* the corporeal meaning, but *in*
it (as I have already said above) the interiority is *directly* experienced in
the body as "corps-je."

[40] Article in *Verbum* 31 (1964), p. 407; see above, footnote 13 of this
chapter.

to analyse the eucharistic presence. He correctly presupposes Christ's presence in the community celebrating the Eucharist: "The Eucharist begins with a *praesentia realis* . . . and its aim is to make this presence more intimate."[41] Indeed, anyone who denies this context is bound to misunderstand transubstantiation and make it too "objective." The signs of the eucharistic bread only imply a presence as an offer, emanating from the Lord in his assembled community. The "real presence" that is peculiar to the Eucharist is thus confined to the category of *personal* presence. "It is interpersonal—the host mediates between the Lord (in his Church) and me (in the same Church). I kneel, not before a Christ who is, as it were, condensed in the host, but before the Lord himself who is offering his reality, his body, to me through the host."[42] The host is Christ's gift of himself, and Christ's presence is that of the giver in the gift, as J. Möller and, later, L. Smits have argued. The gift here is food and drink, but these are not a gift from an *ordinary* man, but from Jesus, the Christ, and they are therefore the nondeceptive, but irrevocably authentic gift of Christ himself. It is, of course, true that Christ also gives himself in the other sacraments. But his gift of himself is realised in the most supreme way in the Eucharist—the bread and the wine become fully *signs*. "What takes place in the Eucharist is a change of sign." Transubstantiation is a transfinalisation or a transsignification, but at a depth which only Christ reaches in his most real gift of himself. Bread and wine become

[41] *Ibid.*, p. 413.
[42] *Ibid.*, p. 414.

(together with the words of consecration) the signs which realise this most deep gift of Christ himself.[43] Schoonenberg concludes: "Those among us who are older rightly regard their faith in Christ's presence under the species as a great treasure. This treasure is not taken away from them when . . . this presence of Christ under the species is situated entirely within his presence in the community."[44]

It is not really necessary to discuss L. Smits' argument separately, as it follows, with a few different shades of meaning, the same basic direction as that of Schoonenberg. He was anxious to find an example which would make it clear that, in our civilisation, a "banquet" tends to develop into a ceremony in which the eating and drinking proper are pushed into the background. His real intentions here were, however, not understood, with the result that he was unjustly regarded, outside the Netherlands especially, as having put forward a kind of "theology of the eucharistic visit." He himself, however, only intended this visit, in which tea and a biscuit were offered, as a suggestive example. His central idea too was the *uniqueness* of *Christ's* giving of himself in the gift of bread and wine.[45]

---

[43] *Ibid.*, p. 415.

[44] *Ibid.*

[45] Two recent studies, which I can do no more than mention here, came to my attention after I had finished writing this book. These are E. Gutwenger's "Das Geheimnis der Gegenwart Christi in der Eucharistie," *Zts. f. Kath. Theol.* 88 (1966), pp. 185–97, and E. Pousset's "L'Eucharistie: présence réelle et transsubstantiation," *Rech. Sc. Rel.* 54 (1966), pp. 177–212.

The Distinctively Eucharistic Manner of the "Real Presence"

The authentic context in which the Eucharist should be seen has been very suggestively described by Schoonenberg and Davis especially. I postulate this as well-known—and central—and should like now only to consider *specific* problems more fully.

Biblical Assumptions

As I am not a professional exegete, I must not allow myself to be seduced into agreeing completely with the interpretation of the biblical texts on the Eucharist put forward by the Lutheran exegete Willi Marxsen.[46] I should, however, like to draw attention with some emphasis to certain points contained in his analysis and, in that case, must also mention a study by B. van Iersel which appeared before Marxsen's books and which is in fact complementary to his work.[47] If the arguments which claim that the Pauline tradition is older than that of Mark are accepted, then it is clear that the development of the interpretation of the "celebration of a meal with Jesus" in the primitive Church was parallel to that of a progressive penetration into the mystery of Christ. Originally, the emphasis was not on *interpreting*

[46] *Das Abendmahl als christologisches Problem*, Gütersloh (1963); see also *Anfangsprobleme der Christologie*, Gütersloh (1964).

[47] See above, Chapter I, footnote 53.

this meal, but on celebrating and experiencing it. In celebrating this meal, early Christians had the experience of
being a Church—an eschatological community on the basis
of their personal relationship with Jesus, whom they had
come to know explicitly as the Christ in the resurrection.
This personal relationship with Jesus—concretely expressed in
community with him at table—was experienced then as a
christological and therefore as an eschatological relationship—as being placed before the living God. The primitive
Church had the experience of being an eschatological *community,* the people of the New Covenant, on the way to the
kingdom of God, in and by celebrating the fraternal meal,
as had happened before when Jesus was still on earth. The
deep meaning of this shared Christian meal was indicated
by the words that were spoken over the bread at the beginning of the meal and over the wine at the end—this community in Christ determined the relationship towards the
kingdom of God. The personal relationship with Christ
which was experienced in faith in this Christian fellowship
was explicitly pointed at in the liturgical words pronounced
over the bread and the wine. They expressed what the personal relationship—the community at table—with Jesus
meant to the primitive Church and continued to mean after
his departure—namely, his real presence in the assembled
community. Jesus had died, but his followers had the visible
experience of his continued life and active presence among
them, because they, the believers, formed one community
by virtue of his death "for our sins" and his resurrection.

This earliest interpretation was further elaborated in the

tradition of Mark, in which Christ, united to the eschatological community, was explicitly associated with the food
and drink consumed by the community that was united in
Christ. The meaning of the community with Christ at table
was here preserved only in the words pronounced over the
bread and wine and in the partaking of this bread and wine.
Christ's real presence in his community was concentrated
cultically in his real presence under the forms of bread and
wine. This was a legitimate development within the New
Testament itself, but it threatened to become one-sided because the eschatological existence of the believing community, in their special relationship with Jesus as realised in
their community with him at table, was thus pushed into
the background. Even in the New Testament, then, the
emphasis was transferred from the ecclesiastical community
of grace in Christ (the *res sacramenti*) to the real presence
of Christ in the Eucharist under the species of bread and
wine (the *res et sacramentum*). The eschatological orientation was now experienced in a cultic event which effectively
expressed the deepest meaning of the continuing history.

This progressive interpretation in the primitive Church—
safeguarded by the interpretation and the preservation of the
Holy Spirit—thus shows that, in the continuing life of the
Church, the real presence of Christ in the Eucharist was subordinated to the eschatological personal community with
the Lord who had really died, but who continued, on the
basis of his real resurrection, as God's saving act, to be effective in his community. It was ultimately a question of the
eschatological personal bond with the living Lord, and the

celebration of the Eucharist anticipated this as an effective sign. The *sōma Christou* was de facto really experienced in this meal.

Like these early Christians, we too must experience this reality within the concrete context of our contemporary lives by constantly making present and reinterpreting here and now, by giving new life to, what these first Christians experienced in contact with the living Christ. The past is also a call to us now, a word that the glorified Christ addresses to *us,* whose situation is equally characterised by his death and resurrection and his sending of the Holy Spirit. It is a call to us to realise a fraternal community by participating in a Christian meal. The living Christ identifies himself with the community at table, he himself becomes the food and drink that is offered at the meal, and we can live in this community from his redeeming death and his being raised to power by the Father.

This is sufficient for Christian *life.* This seems to me to be the meaning of the declaration made by the Dutch bishops, in their pastoral letter on the Eucharist, leaving further interpretation to theologians.[48] This requires a hesitant and reverent approach not only to the original New Testament datum, but also to the elaboration of this datum in the later Church under the guarantee of the Holy Spirit. The witness of the apostles must therefore be our guiding principle in this, and not phenomenology directly. But the basic meaning of this apostolic witness can only be preserved for us in a

---

[48] *Herderlijk Schrijven van het Nederlands episcopaat over de eucharistie* (9 May, 1965). See *Kath. Arch.* 20 (1965), pp. 598–600.

pure state if it is viewed from our present context of life and thus approached phenomenologically. In this perspective, then, I should like to put forward a few supplementary data which are, in my opinion, necessary if the original inviolable datum of the Catholic confession of faith is to be reinterpreted in a way that is faithful to the tradition of the Church.

The Basic Principle: Reality Is Not Man's Handiwork

The Basis of All Man's Giving of Meaning. In the Eucharist, "the Lord's death is proclaimed" (1 Cor. 11. 26). This context cannot be overlooked in any existential or phenomenological approach without misrepresenting the mystery of the Eucharist. Christ is present in the Eucharist as the Lord—that is, as the one who gave himself in death "for our sins" and was brought to life for us by God. Our personal relationship with the Lord is also essentially an *anamnēsis,* a calling to mind of the historical event of salvation on the cross, not insofar as it is past, but insofar as it endures eternally in its completion. The eternity is, however, not situated behind history, but accomplished in history, and the ultimate completion is the closing of history, not by leaving history behind, but by bestowing a lasting validity on this history itself, namely in its completion. That is why our relationship to the risen Christ is identical with our relationship to the historical Jesus.

Because of the eucharistic context, a "real presence" can never be viewed in isolation. It is clear from the words "Take and eat, this is my body" that a *meal* was constituted a sacrament, not simply food and drink, bread and wine, although these form an inward aspect of the sacrament. The crucified, dead and risen Lord becomes really present in a meal. He gives his death and resurrection as a meal, and this is therefore at the same time an *anamnesis,* a remembrance.

What, then, is the distinctively eucharistic meaning, within this context, of the "real presence"?

Several modern authors correctly regard the creation, the beginning of the covenant of grace, as the background to the eucharistic event as well. For the believer, things are not only what they are in themselves and what man experiences of them in his life within this world. For him, they are, in accordance with their own measure of being, also divine revelation. As a subject standing, because of his own bodiliness, in the midst of the material world, man is the centre of the world and thus, at the same time, the subject in which God's revelation finds a response, is received and interpreted. What is more, this response to and reception and interpretation of revelation takes place in and through what things are themselves. Creation is a divine act which cannot, of its very nature, be directed towards God's completion of himself, but is God's pure and gratuitous communication of himself, his love for his creatures. In concrete terms, it is God's love for man in the world. God's creation thus establishes a personal presence of God in all things (which are there for man—God's gifts to man) and especially in the subject that is called man, to whom these gifts are given out of love. In what they are, things *are,* through God's creative will, really saving values and divine revelation, revealing and veiling at the same time, and they are this both metaphysically and really, and not only in the minds of those who believe, even though someone who does not believe cannot recognise this reality of being, at least in his thematic consciousness. In this sense, it is therefore possible to say that the entire world has a general quasi-sacramental significance. This Christian view of creation does not empty matter of its proper meaning, but renders it intelligible in its deepest meaning. For the believer, the function secular reality has as a *sign* is deeply involved with its *concrete being.*

This has far-reaching consequences for our human knowledge. We confront the world as giving it meaning, certainly, but it is not our handiwork. It is given to us by God as our world. Man, it is true, leads an essentially interpretative existence which to some extent allows light to be thrown on reality—that is, on truth—which presents it precisely as intelligible. But the meanings given by man are governed by a reality which is (not chronologically, but in metaphysical priority) in the first place God's, and only then man's. That is why reality is a *mystery,* the form, disclosing and concealing at the same time, in which God reveals himself. The deepest essence of persons and things therefore always escapes us. Thus our knowledge, which both takes and gives meaning, can only grasp reality insofar as the explicit content of knowledge refers to the mystery which eludes us and is always beyond our grasp. We live in a reality which is given to us as God's gift. We live as strangers in this reality, yet we are at the same time invited to accept it, and we therefore experience it explicitly as a mystery and thus as a gift. But it is in this reality that we are permitted to live and to discover our well-being.

This reality, so difficult to penetrate, in which we live and which we ourselves also are, is the fertile soil of our life of giving meaning. The referential character of our consciousness is therefore essential. As believers, we know that all this is traceable to God's giving, *personal real presence,* which we experience in the shadow that this presence throws on the creaturely reality. Everything that is explicit in our consciousness is therefore only referential, referring to the mystery. We know reality only in signs. Thus, what we consciously experience as bread and wine is also always a sign of the reality which escapes us, even outside the context of the Eucharist. Everything pertaining to things thus always conceals a personal relationship for us. God's personal presence is always the deepest relationship *in everything*—it situates us within the mystery in which we are invited to give a human meaning. The fundamental meaning for me is a gift of the reality itself, which is originally not *my* reality, but is nonetheless given to me for me to give meaning to it.

Because of this fundamental meaning for me, I can go on to establish various meanings which will determine what things signify concretely for me on the basis of what they are themselves. I cannot set about this task arbitrarily, because I am at the same time tied to the reality given to me. Situated within the mystery that is given to me, however, I *establish* a human world, the human meaning of which I am continuously changing. It is only the human meaning of the world that I can change, however, since its deepest, metaphysical meaning is beyond human understanding and intervention.

I propose now gradually to develop this basic idea in connection with the Eucharist. In this, I shall proceed from the more superficial level to greater depth, so that the decisive question—whether transubstantiation and transsignification are identical or not—will be asked and answered last of all.

Human Giving of Meaning—Productive and Symbolic. Man is able to improve certain natural elements by natural processes—he has, for example, in this way obtained wheat, from which he is able, by technical means, to make bread. Wine is similarly the end product of natural and technical processes. In this sense, then, bread and wine are, as products of human cultivation and techniques, the result of a human activity of giving purpose, for the benefit of *man* and for his use. But this giving of purpose by man can and does go further than this.

Bread and wine, already useful to man as nourishing physical life, have a further function in human intercourse. They have a symbolic meaning—bread is the symbol of life and wine is the symbol of the joy of life. Products of human cultivation can therefore be given all kinds of relative meanings at different levels. In the case of men sharing a meal together at table, eating and drinking, already in themselves useful biologically, can be raised to a higher level of human good.

They can become the expression of fraternal solidarity, of interpersonal intimacy, of the successful conclusion of an agreement or a treaty or of the sealing of a friendship. Because man in fact lives in a *humanised* world, he is above all concerned with this kind of human giving of meaning—he lives in them and from them, within the mystery of the reality which he cannot himself create, but which has been given to him.

The biological utility of eating and drinking is not denied by this further meaning, but is included in a specifically human event. An animal's eating is *essentially* different from a man's eating, even though the biological process is the same. A thing can become essentially different without being physically or biologically changed. In interpersonal relationships, bread acquires a completely different meaning from that which it has for the physicist or the metaphysician, for example. Remaining physically what it is, bread can be included in a sphere of meaning that is quite different from the purely biological. In that case, the bread *is* different, because the definite relationship to man at the same time defines the reality under discussion. Of course, man lives in fact from continuous "transsignifications"—he humanises the world. And such changes of meaning are more radical than purely physical changes, which are at a lower level and, in this sense, at a less real level. Establishing meaning is more than a psychic intention. There is an essential correlation between the object, the bread, and the subject, the meaning given by man, within the *mystery* of the reality in which the world is given to us and we are given to ourselves. The change of meaning is accomplished precisely in the *human-ised* world and in this context it is a substantial change.

It is remarkable how the word "transubstantiation" has seemed to suggest this phenomenon to poets and in the poetic liturgy of the Church. In a letter to his beloved, Goethe, for example, said, "For me, you are transubstantiated into all objects,"[49] implying that he experienced her in all the things that surrounded him in everyday life, that plants and trees, flowers and fruit were different for him—the sphere of meaning of an interpersonal communion, the realising sign of the presence of his beloved. This giving of meaning is in contact with a human reality and is not a dream (although it could also be a dream—in human life, "reality" is infinitely varied). Within the sphere of this particular experience of reality, things are different from what they would be in another sphere of experience. It should, however, be remembered that, in this case, it is a question of man's relative attitudes to the world and that the basic assumption that the *being* of reality is *given* and is, in its own being, meaningful to man (*ens et bonum convertuntur*) remains. This preliminary and basic meaning makes man's giving of relative meanings possible and invites it.

In describing the distinctive reality of a definite human datum, it is important not to jump from one level to another. On the basis of these general remarks, it is therefore necessary to say that, even apart from the specifically Christian

[49] "Du bist mir in alle Gegenstände transsubstanziiert," *Goethe erzählt sein Leben* (Furche Bücherei, no. 136), Hamburg (n.d.), p. 207.

meaning of the Eucharist, a *positive* answer to the question, "Is the bread still *ordinary bread* after the consecration?" is completely meaningless. This is simply jumping from the cultic level to that of, for example, the physicist. It is, of course, possible to ask about the physical reality, but an answer to this question must not be thought of as an answer to the cultic and, in this case, theological question. Confusion of this kind—it is, of course, much more than simply a manner of speaking—has obscured all questions concerning the Eucharist. The answer to a question asked in a eucharistic context ("What is the form of bread *after the consecration?*") can only be eucharistic. The answer given by a physicist or a chemist who is concerned with atoms and molecules may perhaps teach us something indirectly, but it will ultimately be irrelevant to the Eucharist. The Tridentine statement is therefore, apart from its specifically Catholic significance, first and foremost a denial that the bread can still be called bread after the consecration. For the Eucharist as such, it is a question precisely of this. A further analysis of what the bread is, for example, physically or metaphysically, outside this context, is irrelevant.

On the basis of these general principles, it is therefore possible to say that eucharistic transubstantiation cannot be viewed in isolation from the sphere of giving meaning in sacramental signs. Because of the paschal context ("Take and eat, this is my body"), it must moreover be situated within the sphere of reality of Christ's *gift of himself* that is meaningful and capable of being experienced, a remembrance, both doing and speaking, of Christ's death and resurrection. The level of physics and the philosophy of nature can therefore be disregarded. Transubstantiation is inseparably a "human"[50] *establishment of meaning*. I have, however, not yet said anything about the question of whether transubstantiation and transsignification are identical. I have, on the other hand, ruled out the view that only *our attitude towards* a datum that remains unchanged is changed in the Eucharist.[51]

The Eucharist and "Bread and Wine" in Human Religious Symbolic Activity. When bread and wine were given their place in the Eucharist, their human significance had already been changed. In the first place, they were not simply raw natural elements, but products of human cultivation with an inseparable relationship to man. They were essentially and substantially objects of biological utility, intended as nourishment for man. They were then included, in a human manner, in the meal and thus acquired a function in human fellowship. The primary sacramental form of the Eucharist is therefore not simply "bread and wine," but the *meal* in which bread and wine are consumed. Sacraments are, after all, never isolated things, but human actions, in which things or gestures are included, for example, *washing with* water, *anointing with* oil, *laying on* of hands and so on. Thus, in the Eucharist, the food, the meal and the community of be-

[50] I shall define more precisely what I mean by "human" later on.

[51] See E. Le Roy, *Dogme et critique,* Paris (1907), p. 20. Le Roy interpreted transubstantiation, as he did every dogma, pragmatically.

lievers at table all essentially belong to each other—they are the *human* matter which becomes sacrament.

A great deal, however, had preceded the Eucharist. Bread and wine (or equivalent food)[52] had become the symbol of life and had therefore acquired a place in the worship of the natural religions, in which God was experienced as the origin of all life, and especially in the so-called "cosmic liturgy," in which thanks were given to God for his good gifts of life. In Israel, these feasts were given a foundation in history, because Yahweh had not revealed himself primarily as the God of nature, but as the God of history, who had even forced nature to serve the history of his people. Israel's paschal feast was therefore the liturgical remembrance of an event of salvation, an *anamnēsis* of the exodus from Egypt, Yahweh's deliverance of his people.

The cosmic cult and Israel's liturgy of Yahweh's history of salvation with his people came together in the Eucharist, achieving their inward but transcendental fulfilment in something that was quite simply entirely new. The primitive Church situated the Eucharist within the context of the Old Testament paschal celebration (with different emphases in

---

[52] According to historians of biology, the bread that Jesus used in his daily life had little to do with the wheaten bread that we have come to use in the West since the sixteenth century and, biologically, wine is nothing more or less than currant juice (according to my colleague, the botanist, Dr. H. F. Linskens). For this reason alone, theologians ought to be more discreet about the "matter" of the Eucharist which is now firmly established in clearly defined principles. Is the use of bread and wine of *dogmatic* significance for the concrete celebration of the Eucharist simply because Christ used bread and wine?

the various sources) and also used the paschal bread, but she did this in the perspective of the new Passover, the definitive event of redemption—Christ's sacrificial death and his resurrection. What the gospels say is, This bread—both the symbol of life (*de tuis donis ac datis*—the cosmic liturgy) and the paschal bread (the Old Testament liturgy with its historical significance)—is my body. My body is a paschal sacrifice which I give you here to eat. "I am the Life"—this is what is really experienced in the Eucharist, in *anamnēsis* of the Lord who died, but is living.

The transubstantiation that is implied in this context clearly evokes a reality at a very definite level. The level is that of the celebration of a meal, a meal that is celebrated in a religious symbolic activity—that is, in a rite which *asks for life* and which *gives life* and which is a recollection of the living sacrifice or the "death of the Lord." The bread and the wine which are involved in this activity are not simply a hospitable gift at a visit. The idea of a "visit" made by Christ to the elements is alien to the Eucharist. What happens in the Eucharist is that the faithful share in Christ's rising to life and accomplish this with him in faith while giving thanks to God. It is precisely to this that Christ's "real presence" in the Eucharist relates. There is, for example, not directly a presence for the purpose of adoration in the Eucharist. The really sacramental element, the *ratio sacramenti,* is precisely our eucharistic accomplishment with Christ of, and salvific inclusion in, the life-giving death of the Lord. "Into thy hands I commend my spirit"—with, in and through Christ (according to the canon of the Roman rite), we commend

our lives into the hands of the Father, in service to man in
the world.

*The Real Presence of Christ and of His Church in the
Eucharist.* The specifically eucharistic "real presence" now
can also be defined more precisely in the perspective of this
specifically eucharistic efficacy of grace. The basis of the
entire eucharistic event is Christ's personal gift of himself to
his fellow-men and, within this, to the Father. This is quite
simply his *essence*—"The man Christ Jesus is the one *giving
himself*" (*ho dous heauton,* 1 Tim. 2. 6). The eternal validity
of his history on earth resides in this. As I have already said,
the personal relationship to the heavenly Christ is at the same
time an *anamnēsis* of his historical death on the Cross.

The Eucharist is the sacramental form of this event,
Christ's giving of himself to the Father and to men. It takes
the form of a commemorative meal in which the usual secular significance of the bread and wine is withdrawn and
these become bearers of Christ's gift of himself—"Take and
eat, this is my body." Christ's gift of himself, however, is not
ultimately directed towards bread and wine, but towards the
faithful. The real presence is intended for believers, but
through the medium of and *in* this gift of bread and wine.
In other words, the Lord who gives himself thus is *sacramentally* present. In this commemorative meal, bread and
wine become the subject of a new *establishment of meaning,*
not by men, but by the living Lord *in* the Church, through
which they become the *sign* of the real presence of Christ
giving himself to us. This establishment of meaning by

Christ is accomplished in the Church and thus presupposes the real presence of the Lord in the Church, in the assembled community of believers and in the one who officiates in the Eucharist.

I should like to place much greater emphasis than most modern authors have done on this essential bond between the real presence of Christ in the Eucharist and his real presence as Lord living in the Church. After all, there is ultimately only one real presence of Christ, although this can come about in various ways. It forms, in my opinion, an essential element in the constitution of the Eucharist. In interpreting the Eucharist, it is not enough simply to consider Christ's presence "in heaven" and "in bread and wine," like the scholastic theologians, who regarded Christ's real presence in the faithful only as the fruit of these two poles, the *res sacramenti*. By virtue of the meaning which is given to them by Christ and to which the Church consents in faith, the bread and wine are really *signs,* a specific sacramental form of the Lord who is already really and personally present for us. If this is denied or overlooked, then the reality of Christ's presence in the Eucharist is in danger of being emptied of meaning. Transubstantiation does not mean that Christ, the Lord living in his Church, gives *something* to us in giving this new meaning, that he, for example, gives us incarnate evidence of love, as in every meaningful present, in which we recognise the hand and indeed the heart of the giver and ultimately therefore experience also the giver himself. No, in transubstantiation, the relationships are at a much deeper level. What is given to us is the giver himself. This gift of the giver himself is quite inadequately rendered by the phenomenological "giving of oneself *in* the gift." "This is my body, this is my blood": this is not a giving of oneself in a gift, not even at a more profound level because the giver here is Christ, the personal revelation of the Father. No, what is given to us in the Eucharist is *nothing other than Christ himself*. What the sacramental forms of bread and wine signify, and at the same time make real, is not a gift that refers to Christ who gives himself in them, but Christ himself in living, personal presence. The signifying function of the sacrament (*sacramentum est in genere signi*) is here at its highest value. It is a making present of himself of the real, living Christ in a pure, meaningful presence which we are able to experience in faith. The phenomenal form of the eucharistic bread and wine is nothing other than the *sign* which makes real Christ's gift of himself with the Church's responding gift of herself involved in this making real to us, a sign inviting every believer to participate personally in this event.

The sacramental bread and wine are therefore not only the sign which makes Christ's presence real to us, but also the sign bringing about the real presence of the Church (and, in the Church, of us too) to him. The eucharistic meal thus signifies both Christ's gift of himself and the Church's responding gift of herself, of the Church who is what she is in him and can give what she gives in and through him. The sacramental form thus signifies the *reciprocity* of the "real presence." As the definitive community of salvation, the Church cannot be separated from Christ. If, then, Christ makes himself present in this particular sacrament, the Church also makes herself present at the same time. The presence of both Christ and his Church is meaningfully expressed in this sacramental sign in common surrender to the Father "for the salvation of the whole world" and thus realised in a special way. This is why Augustine was able to say that "we ourselves lie on the paten" and the whole patristic and scholastic tradition was able to call the Eucharist the "sacrament of the unity of the Church with Christ." "This is my body" is "the body of the Lord," the New Covenant, the unity of the Church with Christ. "Because there is one bread, we who are many are one body, for we all partake of the one bread" (I Cor. 10. 17). This does not do away with the real presence of Christ himself, which is, of course, the foundation of the Church. The "body of the Lord" in the christological sense is the source of the "body of the Lord" in the ecclesiological sense. Christ's "eucharistic body" is the community of the two—the reciprocal real presence of Christ and his Church, meaningfully signified sacramentally in the *nourishing* of the "body that is the Church" by Christ's body.

In the Eucharist, then, the new, definitive covenant is celebrated and made present in the community. Priority must be given to Christ in the Eucharist. In the Middle Ages, the really present body of Christ (*res et sacramentum*) was traditionally taken as the point of departure and the really present "body that is the Church" was only considered in the second place. But Christ's real presence to his Church and the Church's real presence to her Lord are really "sacramentalised" in the Eucharist, with the result that this reciprocal real presence becomes deeper and more intimate in and because of the sacramental form and that the *reciprocal* giving of self to the Father in the form of a gift of love to fellow-men becomes, through this celebration, more firmly rooted in the saving event of Christ's death and resurrection. Thus the Eucharist is directed towards the *Father,* "with, in and through Christ," and towards *fellow-men* in fraternal love and service. The Eucharist forms the Church and is the bringing about of herself of the Church which lives from the death and resurrection of Christ.[53]

All this has important consequences for the constitution of the Eucharist and for transubstantiation. The presence offered by Christ in the Eucharist naturally precedes the individual's acceptance of this presence and is not the result of it. It therefore remains an offered *reality,* even if I do not respond to it. My disbelief cannot nullify the reality of Christ's real offer and the reality of the Church's remaining in Christ. But, on the other hand, the eucharistic real presence also includes, in its sacramentality itself, reciprocity and is therefore completely realised only when consent is given in faith to the eucharistic event and when this event is at the same time accomplished personally, that is, when this reciprocity takes place, in accordance with the true meaning of the sign, in the sacramental meal.

The eucharistic presence is therefore not dependent on the faith of the individual, but the sacramental offer cannot be

---

[53] According to Thomas, the bread and wine in the Eucharist are *ultimately* signs of Christ's real presence *in the faithful.* See *ST,* III, q. 73, a. 1, 3 and 6.

thought of as separate from the community of the Church. It is, after all, a real presence of Christ *and of his Church*.[54] As the scholastic theologians correctly said, the Eucharist was constituted in its sacramentality, not by the faith of the individual, but, thanks to the intention of the celebrating priest as expressed in the rite of consecration, by the "faith of the Church."[55] It is correct to say that the Eucharist is a rite of the Church and the real presence of Christ living in the Church. It implies a "human" giving of meaning which does not, however, come from man, but from the Lord living in the Church or from the Church as living in the Lord. This giving of meaning can therefore only take place within the sphere of the "faith of the Church" in the Lord who really lives and is present in the Church. This does not make transubstantiation any less real or reduce it to a purely subjective or intentional event. It does, however, mean that the eucha-

[54] On the basis of the presence of both Christ and his Church, the *liturgical* form of the Eucharist requires the presence of a believing community. The *dogmatic* form of the "real presence" of the people of God is undoubtedly preserved in the so-called "private mass," namely in the consecrated signs ("which we are," as Augustine said), but, if there is no real community celebrating mass together with the priest, the possibility of a liturgical experience of this reciprocal real presence is reduced to a minimum!

[55] See, for example, Thomas, *In IV Sent.*, d. 1, q. 1, a. 4, sol. 3, c. and ad 3: "Huic autem causae (sc. Deo) continuatur per *fidem Ecclesiae* quae et instrumentum refert ad principalem causam et signum ad significatum" and Bonaventure, *In IV Sent.*, d. 6, p. 2, a. 2, q. 1, ad 2: "Intentio est necessaria qua copulatur actus ille *fidei Ecclesiae* tamquam actus particularis" (ed. Quaracchi, pt. 4, p. 153). These statements must, of course, be considered within the context of the medieval understanding of the eucharistic presence.

ristic reality can only be approached from faith and is therefore not valid as a reality for a non-believer because he simply
has not reached this level of reality. But this disbelief does
not nullify the reality of the Eucharist.

If, however, we try to objectivise the consecrated bread to
such a point that it becomes dissociated from the faith of the
Church, then it becomes incapable of being experienced and
indeed meaningless.[56] Christ's real presence in the Eucharist
is, of course, *really* an offer of grace, independent of the individual's faith. But the eucharistic liturgy is also an event
which establishes meaning and the significance of the eucharistic bread and wine cannot be determined apart from this.
All physical or metaphysical interpretation which takes place
outside the sphere of sacramentality is valueless as far as our
understanding of the Eucharist is concerned. When anything
untoward happens to a consecrated host, but no believer is,
or could remotely be, involved in the incident, it does not
matter. If, for example, we hear that a mouse has nibbled at
it, we need not be alarmed—the level of reality with which
the Eucharist is concerned can only be reached by the believer as a *reality* even though its existence is not dependent
on the faith of the individual.[57] What then, the "faith of the

[56] What is generally valid: "un au-delà de la pensée est impensable"
here becomes "un au-delà de la foi est incroyable."

[57] Because the species of bread is—at the level of the *reality,* which,
after all, has meaning only for man and, in this case, only for believing
man—the sign of Christ's offered real presence, believing *man* will, of
course, try to prevent such things from happening out of reverence, as it
has a significance for *him* because reality is meaningful for him. On the
basis of this, sacramentally in the second place, the reverence which sur-

Church" realises in the coming about of Christ's eucharistic presence as a sacramental offer, the faith of the individual realises in his personal acceptance of this offered presence. The Church's relationship within the Covenant with Christ realises the "sacramental sign," whereas the individual person's attitude in faith within the believing community realises his personal involvement in this Covenant.

Transubstantiation and Transsignification or a New Giving of Meaning

It is only against the background of the whole eucharistic event, as outlined briefly in the foregoing paragraphs, that attention can be focussed on the question, "What *is*, then, that eucharistic bread and wine in the last resort?" The non-Christian cannot see any change whatever, and even the believer cannot see any difference if without his noticing it consecrated hosts are replaced by unconsecrated hosts.

In the very first place, this points clearly to the fact that the bread and wine cannot be dissociated from the rite of the

---

rounds the reservation of the Eucharist also becomes meaningful and even a eucharistic duty in the human and Christian sense. The words of the New Covenant are pronounced over this bread and Christ's offer of grace remains real in it so long as it remains a "sign"; so long, in other words, as the bread is, in the human sense, nourishment—that is, edible. Such traditional ceremonies as those which take place around consecrated wine spilt on the altar-cloth seem to me exaggerations. It is no longer possible to drink the spilt wine and consequently this has very little more to do with the *sacrament*.

Eucharist. This is why even the reservation of the hosts is so surrounded by marks of reverence that the eucharistic context is clearly preserved. But this poses the question as to whether this reverence is sufficiently explicable on the basis of the Church's transsignification of the meal. And with this, we are approaching the final question—is transsignification identical with transubstantiation, or is it a consequence or an implication of transubstantiation? The question that arises here in its full extent is that of reality.

Reality and Its Phenomenal Appearance. The question we have to ask ourselves is ultimately, What is the *reality* that we experience in our perception of the eucharistic form? We cannot therefore avoid briefly situating the structure of human perception.

Human perception—and I am speaking here only of man —has a very specific unity, that of a spiritual act (that is, of active openness to reality) with what is perceived by the senses. As such, sensory perception (that is, what is percevied by the senses *and* perception) cannot be called either objective or subjective and should not be interpreted either realistically or idealistically. What is perceived cannot be separated from the subject who perceives it. It is not independent of the environment that appeals to man and is therefore not purely a condition of the consciousness. It is also not independent of the reaction of a subject and is therefore not an objective quality of reality.[58] What this naturally implies, then, is that anything that has meaning for sensory percep-

[58] See E. Strauss, *Vom Sinn der Sinne*, Berlin (1956²).

tion is bound to lose this meaning if divorced from this perception. This has been clearly illustrated by Merleau-Ponty, who was, however, inclined to apply it to human consciousness in its totality.

Purely sensory perception, however, does not occur in man. He sees, hears, smells, tastes and touches in a *human* manner, and thus humanises both what he perceives and perception. Perception, which, as such, only serves biological utility, is therefore (together with its content) included in the orientation of the human spirit towards reality, the sphere of the specifically human, the *honestum,* what ultimately is—the world as the reality of God which we are permitted to enter. Thus perception (together with its content) is raised above purely sensory relativity and taken in the direction of the spiritual meaning of reality. It therefore refers externally, as in signs, to reality itself which, as such, only has meaning for the human spirit. In this sense, man himself fashions the signifying function that the content of his perception has with regard to reality and makes this content a referential sign. Despite his complexity, man is nonetheless a unity and all his conscious orientation towards reality must therefore be clothed in and borne up by referential sensory perception of this kind. The human spirit cannot approach the mystery of the reality that is constantly escaping him without these references of (humanly qualified) sensory perception. In this sense, our entire human consciousness is situated *in* human perception, and not behind, above or beneath it. The sensory contents which we acquire in vital contact with our environment (in our case, bread and wine) cannot be regarded as an objective qualification of reality. They can therefore neither be called accidents nor objective attributes of a "substance" which is, so to speak, situated at a deeper level. It therefore seems that to make an Aristotelian distinction between substance and accidents cannot help us in interpreting the dogma of transubstantiation.

Partly through sensory perception, man opens himself up to the mystery of reality, to the metaphysical being which is prior to and is offered to man's ontological sense—that is, to his logos, which *makes* being *appear* and thus *establishes meaning*. This previously given reality is not man's handiwork. Reality is never this—it is God's creation. The dogma of creation and the metaphysical realism that is the consequence of this dogma are at the centre of all theological speculation. The reality of creation is necessarily prior to all giving of meaning by man. It is only within this already given mystery, and only if man builds upon the inviolable but mysterious gift which the "world of God" is, that man, giving meaning, can make a *human* world for himself.

Man's condition, however—his life of the senses, his conceptual approach and his concrete association with things— also determines the way in which reality *appears*. A certain difference between reality itself and its phenomenal appearance results from this human condition. The reality does not, of course, situate itself behind its phenomenal appearance— the appearance is the reality itself. But this appearance is, as such, also coloured by the complex way in which man approaches reality, the consequence of his complex mode of being. The human logos, man's own giving of meaning, thus plays a part in the appearance of reality. The inadequacy of man's knowledge of reality accounts for a certain difference between reality and its appearance as a phenomenon. In this sense, the phenomenal is the *sign* of the reality—it signifies reality. In this context, then, the "phenomenal" includes not only the sensory, but also everything that is *expressed* of the reality itself or concretely appears to us, which is, then, inadequate to what is expressed (the reality as a mystery). Explicit knowledge of reality is therefore a complex unity, in which an *active* openness to what communicates itself as reality is accompanied by a *giving of meaning*. What in fact shows itself to me, however, also acts as a norm for the meaning I give to the reality.

The "Body of the Lord" Appearing in Sacramental Form. It is impossible to neglect the general structure of man's knowledge of reality in thematising the Catholic belief in the real presence of Christ in the Eucharist. To do so would be to make a man's faith into a kind of "superstructure," built on top of our human knowledge. Our understanding in faith of a reality of salvation is also a very complex whole. As I have already pointed out, an active openness in faith to what is objectively communicated to us as reality is accompanied by a giving of meaning in faith, as here too the *appearance* of the reality of salvation is coloured by (believing) man's complex mode of being.

If reality (in the potent sense of "what really *is*") is not man's handiwork and cannot be traced back to a human giving of meaning, but only to God's gift of creation, and if

it is clear from the entire tradition of faith and from the
Tridentine dogma of the Eucharist that the Church, in her
consciousness of faith, strongly insists on the *reality* of the
presence of Christ in the Eucharist, then it must be clear to
the Catholic theologian that eucharistic transsignification is
not identical with transubstantiation, but is intimately connected with it.

It is particularly in the case of the Eucharist that we are
bound to consider the distinction between the reality itself
and this reality as a phenomenal appearance. Normally, of
course, we give no attention to this distinction, and the fact
that we overlook it does not affect our practical lives at all.
But when we reflect about the Eucharist, our noses are, so to
speak, pushed into it. *What* appears, in our experience, as
bread and wine *is* the "body of the Lord" appearing to us (as
sacramental nourishment). The significance of the phenomenal forms of bread and wine changes *because* by the power
of the creative Spirit, the reality to which the phenomenal
refers is changed—it *is* no longer bread and wine, but
nothing less than the "body of the Lord," offered to me as
spiritual nourishment. Because what is signified via the phenomenal is changed objectively, the significance of the phenomenal itself is also changed. Believing man is naturally
involved in this transsignification of the phenomenal. The
new significance of the form of bread and wine means that
the believer actively gives the phenomenal a place in his
orientation towards, and his openness to, *what* really appears
—the "body of the Lord" in the sacramental form of nourishment. In the Eucharist, transubstantiation (*conversio entis—*

what *is* the present reality? Christ's body) and transsignification (the giving of a new meaning or new sign) are indissolubly connected, but it is *impossible simply* to identify
them. The active giving of meaning in faith by the Church
and, with her, by the individual believer takes place within
the mystery of grace of the really present "body of the Lord"
offered by God and attained by the Christian intention to
reach reality. The real presence of Christ in the Eucharist
can therefore only be approached by *allowing* the form of
bread and wine experienced phenomenally to *refer to* this
presence (of Christ and of his Church) in a projective act of
faith which is an *element of and in* faith in Christ's eucharistic presence. The event in which Christ, really present in
the Eucharist, appears, or rather, offers *himself* as food and
in which the believer receives him as food therefore also includes a projective act of faith. This act does not bring about
the real presence, but presupposes it as a metaphysical priority. Thus the "sacramental form" is really the "body of the
Lord" proclaiming itself as food. Christ really gives himself
as food for the believer. This "sacramental form" only
reaches its fulfilment in the meal in which we nourish ourselves on Christ to become a believing community.

I have struggled with the interpretation of this *mysterium
fidei* and, in faithful reverence for what the Catholic *confession* of faith has for centuries allowed Christians to experience in the celebration of the Eucharist, I cannot personally
be satisfied with a *purely* phenomenological interpretation
without metaphysical density. Reality is not man's handi-

work—in this sense, realism is essential to the Christian faith. In my reinterpretation of the Tridentine datum, then, I can never rest content simply with an appeal to a human *giving of meaning alone,* even if this is situated within faith. Of course, a transsignification of this kind has a place in the Eucharist, but it is borne up and evoked by the re-creative activity of the Holy Spirit, the Spirit of Christ sent by the Father. God himself *acts* in the sphere of the actively believing, doing and celebrating Church, and the result of this divine saving activity is sacramentally a "new creation" which perpetuates and deepens our eschatological relationship to the kingdom of God. "The Lord left behind a pledge of this hope and strength for life's journey in that sacrament of faith where natural elements refined by man are changed into His glorified Body and Blood, providing a meal of brotherly solidarity and a foretaste of the heavenly banquet."[59]

[59] "The Pastoral Constitution on the Church in the Modern World," Part I, Ch. III, para. 38, *The Documents of Vatican II,* ed. Walter M. Abbott, S.J. (New York: Guild Press, America Press, Association Press, 1966), pp. 236–237.

CONCLUSION
The "Why" and the "How"

R. KWANT has recently stated that the "how" of transubstantiation is unimportant compared with the "why."[1] It should be clear from my argument in this book, in which I have discussed the "how" within the context of the "why," that I cannot accept this antithesis, unless the intention is that it is meaningless to ask what the bread and wine are after the consecration in the non-eucharistic sense, in other words, apart from the Eucharist. But this ultimately comes down to asking what this reality would be . . . if the Church had *not* pronounced any blessing over the bread and wine!

In referring to a "metaphysical dimension," as, for example, in my conclusion that, according to the Tridentine dogma, this dimension forms an essential part of our faith in Christ's real "presence" in the Eucharist, all I mean is that Christ's eucharistic presence is a *reality*. I am not therefore affirming that this reality is to be found behind the phenomenal appearance, but that it appears *in* the phenomenon to the believer. As a Christian, I believe that it is very important to know whether Christ is merely giving me, in the Eucharist,

[1] "Het 'waarom' is belangrijker dan het 'hoe,'" *De Bazuin* 49 (1965-6), no. 30 (23 April, 1966), pp. 1-2.

a present in which I can taste his love, or whether he is giving me himself as sacramental nourishment. This "how" of the real presence is therefore an answer to a vital Christian question and consequently just as important as the "why."

A new interpretation of the "how" will, of course, only touch the reality inadequately; as such, it cannot provide a definitive formula. We cannot, in our situation in this world, go any farther than this—we can never have absolute possession of the absolute. But this does not mean that it is meaningless to go on speculating about matters of faith from our worldly situation. We are inalienably orientated towards *reality,* which is, by definition, not our handiwork, but which constantly appeals to us. Impelled by this orientation towards reality—and the reality of faith—we have the task of examining and re-examining it and of formulating it for ourselves.

It is also true that our speculation about and our attempts to thematise faith are secondary to our existential experience of the eucharistic event. Yet it can be of service to our experience of the Eucharist, even if only in a preventive sense. Views may emerge from our new understanding of man and the world and develop into a kind of "pre-understanding" that contradicts our interpretive experience and our experiential interpretation of the Eucharist. If we abandon any attempt to reinterpret the Eucharist, we shall then either have to live with a double truth, which will result in an increasing gulf between our lives in the Church and our lives in the world, or else we shall be letting the reality of what we celebrate in faith in the Eucharist sift out imperceptibly. The second course applies at least to our *interpretation* of our experience of the Eucharist, as this experience may itself continue to be orthodox, even though it will, in the long run, be influenced by our interpretation. The danger of this in modern times is not simply imaginary, and it seems to me that the deepest meaning of the encyclical *Mysterium Fidei* is that it points to this as a very real danger. Our present attempts to reinterpret the Tridentine dogma are, on the other hand, simply aimed at providing an answer to this very real tension that is in accordance with the tradition of faith.

Both caution and seeking have a special function in the Church. It is only by means of both that we can hear Christ's original message authentically and at the same time understand it in its contemporary context. Thematisation is, of its very nature, historically coloured and therefore relative, and it is so in the first place because it is related to the modern context of life. In itself, then, relative cannot in any way be equated with irrelevant. Theological thematisation is, after all, also based on what the Church has already expressed concerning faith. Faith cannot simply be identified with orthodox expression, but it is also impossible without content and without some expression. On the other hand, however, it cannot be nailed down to a *definitive* expression or formulation of the datum of faith. It can nonetheless be accepted that the reality of salvation de facto appears in the phenomenal aspect of the life of the Church, for example, in the Church's liturgy and dogma, and yet this phenomenal aspect may still continue to be seen (only) as the appearance of this reality. But we do encounter the reality of salvation *in* the phenomenal aspect of the Church's expressions of faith. In our search for new expressions of faith, we are again and again faced with the question as to whether we are still encountering the reality of faith in these expressions. They cannot guarantee that we shall, unlike the perhaps awkward magisterial expressions of faith made by the Church in the past. Any new interpretation still demands the consent (or possibly rejection) by the faithful, and it has also to be assessed by those who judge all interpretations of faith—the world episcopate in unity with the pope, who themselves live from the gospel of Christ in communion with the entire Church. A new interpretation may be necessary because the old interpretations have ceased to speak to us within our contemporary experience of faith, but anyone who reacts directly *against* an expression of faith that has been dogmatically defined should be extremely critical of himself. Is it, then, so certain that, in attacking the dogmatic formula, full justice is done to the deepest meaning of the datum of faith? Even an interpretation that at first sight appears to be ecumenically more valuable may eventually only harm ecumenism. What is required, in any attempt to reinterpret, is an approach to the reality of salvation that is both diffident and reverent without being either timid or opportunist and a severely critical attitude towards one's own thinking. No single formulation can exhaust the faith, but this does not make every expression of faith true, meaningful or in accordance with faith.

The hermeneutical approach is an urgent matter, but it must not be allowed to become a reason for solipsism in our critical thinking, as though we were able to think out everything afresh from its foundations without any reference to the past and to our own surroundings. Such an attitude would be uncritical and non-existential. The state of being man is not a pure, present "actuality," but an expectation of the future in the present on the basis of the past. Anyone who foresees that his proposal for a new interpretation will give rise to radical misunderstandings and incorrect, unchristian interpretations, will have to be courageous, but also very patient, and will perhaps also have to allow his views to be published gradually. He will have to practise, not paralysing caution, but certainly patience. The impatience that has been displayed in certain quarters seems to me to be an exaggeration of the role of theology in our life of faith.

This does not contradict what I have already said above about the real significance of theological thematisation and the function of the Church's expressions of faith. The theology of the Eucharist will always reveal a certain multiformity, and it may be admitted that, in theological hairsplitting about Christ's real "presence," Christ himself has often been absent! But this does not do away with the fact that orthodoxy, true orientation towards the reality of salvation, is essential to faith, for the very good reason that a Christian does not believe what he pleases, but what God postulates in Christ as the reality of salvation and thus defines as a mystery of faith. Of course man, listening in faith and therefore also interpreting in faith, is himself in history, and his interpretation of what he hears is consequently also coloured by his situation. And this never gives the individual the right to call a fellow-Christian "unorthodox." How can

I judge another's orthodoxy when I myself can have no human or critical certainty about my own orthodoxy and can only firmly *hope* for this by virtue of God's grace?

The constantly growing interpretation of faith by the individual Christian is always exposed to misrepresentation and misinterpretation, but, believing *within* the Church of Christ and sharing in that Church's faith, he is continuously nourished, moulded and corrected by the given reality of salvation itself. This gives him confidence that a new interpretation will, with time, gain the consent of the whole people of God and at the same time encourages him to think that the Church and the world will continue to grow even more afterwards.